Scott Adams and Philosophy

Popular Culture and Philosophy® Series Editor: George A. Reisch

For full details of all Popular Culture and Philosophy® books, visit www.opencourtbooks.com.

Popular Culture and Philosophy®

Scott Adams and Philosophy

A Hole in the Fabric of Reality

EDITED BY

DANIEL YIM, GALEN FORESMAN,
AND ROBERT ARP

OPEN COURT
Chicago

Volume 118 in the series, Popular Culture and Philosophy ®, edited by George A. Reisch

To find out more about Open Court books, visit our website at www.opencourtbooks.com.

Open Court Publishing Company is a division of Carus Publishing Company, dba Cricket Media.

Printed and bound in the United States of America.

Scott Adams and Philosophy: A Hole in the Fabric of Reality

This book has not been prepared, authorized, or endorsed by Scott Adams.

ISBN: 978-0-8126-9977-7

Library of Congress Control Number: 2018946392

This book is also available as an e-book (ISBN 978-0-8126-9983-8).

Contents

Contents

The Reality of Scott Adams

Some philosophers claim that you always know when you're in a dream and when you're awake. But 2016 was a year in which reality often took on a dreamlike quality.

You'd be walking along the street with a friend, engrossed in her phone, and she would suddenly turn and run down a sidestreet, shouting: "Hold on, I've gotta catch this magikarp!" This was the phenomenon of Pokémon GO. News reports told of people who walked off roofs or walked off piers, plummeting to their deaths, in pursuit of wild Pokémon. It hardly seems real, looking back now, but the casualties are still missing.

That wasn't the only strange thing that year. *The Cubs won the World Series!* That seemed to violate some of the laws of physics and mathematics, perhaps even the most fundamental laws of metaphysics. Metaphysicians used to debate whether *not winning* was a necessary or merely a contingent property of the baseball team called the Chicago Cubs. Well, no they didn't, if you take the boring old line that facts matter, but they might have done and they probably thought about it.

Oh yes, and then there was politics. Surely it was high time for a woman president! But, out of nowhere, there came a supernatural surge of support for Bernie Sanders, a dry-as-dust self-proclaimed "socialist," and every trick in the book had to be used to fight off this infuriating challenger. Yes, a few tricks that weren't in the book, too.

On the Republican side, rich entertainment was provided by the entry into the race of the joke candidate, Donald J. Trump. All the most authoritative experts agreed that Trump had absolutely no chance of winning the nomination. In a field of seventeen Republican claimants, Trump was always the center of attention, but obviously, once the field was narrowed, and it became a straight choice between Trump and some more serious candidate, Trump the politician would be flushed down the toilet bowl of history.

In years past, Trump the generic big-city pro-choice liberal had often been tagged as a likely future president, and had been pressed, sympathetically, on this issue by several celebrity media people including no less than Oprah Winfrey. But more recently Trump, following the lead of some of Hillary's supporters in their 2008 primary battles against Obama, had become a proponent of the "birther" theory, that Barack Obama could not legally be president because he was not born in the United States. This gave Trump a different kind of image: a flaky conspiracy crank, pathetically out of the mainstream.

In his pursuit of the Republican nomination, Trump fulfilled the worst expectations—and kept winning. He said the most outrageous things, and wouldn't apologize for them, but somehow, this didn't drive away too many Republican primary voters, and he continued to win primaries. Even the release of an old tape in which Trump boasted that if you were a big celebrity, women would let you grab them by the pussy, somehow failed to dislodge him. Uncharacteristically, on this one occasion Trump issued an apology, and explained that his remark was "locker room talk." He might have said it was *"Game of Thrones* talk," for record millions of Americans were regularly imbibing this epic, filled with words and deeds amid which "grab them by the pussy" would have been way too mild to register even a flicker on the Richter Scale of outrage.

As Trump kept winning, some Democrats began to nurse a delicious fantasy: There was actually a chance Trump might be nominated as the Republican candidate! Then, naturally, Hillary could only win by the most colossal landslide.

One distinguished Republican after another came out as a "never Trumper." So a substantial number of leading *Republicans* were solemnly pledged never to vote for Trump. Demonstrably, that must have sealed his inevitable doom.

Among the many experts who predicted Trump's defeat was Nate Silver, who, especially with his best-selling book, *The Signal and the Noise*, had established himself as a household name for accurate, reliable scientific prediction. Silver pronounced the verdict of statistical science: Trump, with a probability of ninety-eight percent, would lose.

A few days later, Scott Adams, creator of *Dilbert*, the world's most popular cartoon strip, predicted that Trump had a ninety-eight percent chance of winning, yes *winning*, the presidency by a landslide. What?

Adams was politically an ultra-liberal, to the left of Bernie Sanders on most issues and no friend of Trump's policies. Yet he was clearly bowled over and captivated by Trump's personality and behavior. On his blog, Adams kept elaborating and expanding on his prediction of a Trump victory. The blog rapidly gained subscribers, including many Trump supporters, no doubt desperate for any word of hopeful encouragement.

Adams's argument was that Trump was that rare thing, a *Master Persuader*. Adams claimed, and substantiated by detailed analysis, that the apparently wayward and irresponsible things said by Trump were really precisely calibrated "weapons-grade" persuasion technique.

Scott Adams was a trained hypnotist and an enthusiast for the popular "persuasion" literature headed up by Robert Cialdini. One of Adams's key ideas is that people are, overwhelmingly, not rational. They make their most important decisions on purely emotional grounds, and then produce fake "rationalized" stories about why they made those decisions. As a result, when it comes to persuasion, facts really don't matter.

Watching the political game play out, Adams foresaw, not only that Trump would win the presidency, but that his victory would generate a serious mental health problem. Trump was about to "rip a hole in the fabric of reality." The world was about to become darkly alien and incomprehensible to a big segment of Democratic voters. There would be massive emotional distress, "cognitive dissonance," and "mass hysteria." Some folks would need counseling help in coming to terms with what had happened, and Adams saw himself as providing that help in the form of a patient, lucid explanation of the Trump phenomenon. Adams was confident that in office Trump would moderate his policies and effectively govern as a centrist, but this wouldn't placate all of the mentally disturbed Hillary supporters, who would continue to "hallucinate" that horrible Trump was doing horrible things.

Adams, a member of Mensa and long-time dissector of logical fallacies, saw in Trump a highly intelligent and superbly self-controlled individual with a formidable "talent stack." The theory of the talent stack had been developed in Adams's best-selling book, *How to Fail at Almost Everything and Still Win Big: Kind of the Story of My Life*. In this work, Adams kicked aside many of the established platitudes of self-help manuals. He advised his readers to quit their day jobs. He favored "systems" over "goals." In his theory of the talent stack, he argues that success most often comes not from being the absolute best at any one thing, but from being pretty good at a bunch of different things, which could be harnessed together for effectiveness.

Trump won the Republican nomination! Just how big a disaster was this for the Republican Party? Could the Party even survive? All the polls showed, what was obvious anyway, that Trump could only lose catastrophically in the general election . . .

Scott Adams was born in upstate New York in 1957. His family, like many American families, cherished the legend that they had some Native American ancestry, but a recent DNA test has shown this to be untrue. A childhood admirer of the *Peanuts* comic strip, Scott started drawing his own comics at age six, and won a drawing competition at age eleven. In his early twenties, having just got a degree in economics from Hartwick College, he bought a one-way ticket to San Francisco.

Adams went to work for Crocker National Bank and became a bank teller (twice held up at gunpoint), computer programmer, budget analyst, commercial lender, product manager, and supervisor, meanwhile working for his MBA degree from UC Berkeley, and creating *Dilbert*, which he couldn't persuade anyone to publish.

He then moved to Pacific Bell, and at last sold his *Dilbert* cartoon to United Media, who managed to place it in a few publications, giving Adams a small addition to his income. He would get up at 4:00 A.M. to draw his cartoons, and then work a full day at Pacific Bell. Slowly, *Dilbert* became more popular, partly because Adams included his email address in the strip and paid close attention to feedback from fans, modifying the strip to give readers what they most appreciated.

Eventually Scott devoted himself full time to *Dilbert* and in 1996 published *The Dilbert Principle*, his first of several best-selling business books, applying the lessons of *Dilbert* to practical management.

In one irreverent experiment, by arrangement with the CEO of Logitech, Adams wore a wig and a false mustache to impersonate a topnotch business consultant. In this persona, he met with the company's managers and persuaded them to adopt a mission statement that was so impossibly complicated it (quite deliberately) amounted to gibberish.

Scott Adams has written two fiction books on religion, *God's Debris* (2001) and *The Religion War* (2004), followed by selections from his blog wisdom in *Stick to Drawing Comics, Monkey Brain!* (2007) and his how-to-succeed masterpiece *How to Fail at Almost Everything and Still Win Big* (2013).

In *Win Bigly: Persuasion in a World Where Facts Don't Matter* (2017), Scott provides his own account of the 2016 election, his part in it, and his ideas on persuasion. He delivers interactive presentations on Periscope every day, and these are made available on YouTube.

Scott Adams is a provocative and challenging gadfly of popular culture, with a huge and curiously diverse fan following. His work and his ideas are worth examining and criticizing—through the filter of philosophy.

I

In Front of Your Eyes

1
How I Learned to Stop Worrying and Tolerate the Master Persuader Hypothesis

Ivan Wolfe

Warning: this essay discusses Scott Adams, Donald Trump, Socrates, Ancient Greek Sophists, Derren Brown, and some other random items of cultural significance. Try to keep up, and try not to let your own political views cause you to ignore, or otherwise taint, the very serious ideas here. Adams argues that we live in a world where facts don't matter. If you feel they should, you really need to know why they currently don't, and writing Adams off because you think he supports Trump's policies (he mostly doesn't) won't help the current political and rhetorical situation.

Forget All You Know or Think You Know

Far too many of my more progressive friends think Scott Adams is some sort of far-right, alt-right Trump supporter. In fact, too many Trump supporters think the same thing. I have been a semi-fan of Adams since *Dilbert* first appeared, and I have read nearly all his published works, in addition to seeing that he is a witty, clear, and entertaining writer (even when I find his thinking muddled, off base, or outright bizarre). Because of that, when I heard he predicted a landslide victory for Trump (the "Master Persuader hypothesis"), I had two thoughts: 1. He's clearly not predicting this because he supports Trump's policies, and 2. He's crazy wrong.

I thought the first because I had read plenty of Adams's political/religious/philosophical/whatever thoughts, and it seems clear that even Bernie Sanders is somewhere to the right of Adams (there might be specific issues, such as certain types of taxation, where that's not the case, but overall that seems clear). I thought the second because Adams had made some crazy predictions before that have yet to pan out. For example, in *The Dilbert Future* he seriously predicted (based on a somewhat simplistic reading of Thomas S. Kuhn's *The Structure of Scientific Revolutions*) that the theory of evolution would be proven false (though he's somewhat vague on when, implying it would be sometime within the lifetime of the reader; I'm not dead yet, so I guess there's still time). While the prediction was made somewhat humorously, he had a serious point. He meant it as an extreme claim intended to make a point about how science constantly changes and up-dates ideas, concepts, and theories. But—still, evolution proven false? Sounds like a Trump supporter after all, right?

I will admit, I was one of those out of touch elites (I have a PhD after all) who thought Trump had no chance, wouldn't even make it out of the Republican primaries, let alone win (or even come close) in the general election. Well, Adams turned out to be more correct than I was—even modifying his thesis as more scandals and revelations about Trump came out in the media—whereas I stuck firmly to my belief that Trump had no solid chance of winning.

In the interests of full disclosure, I will state that I did not vote for Trump, but I'm going to try to make this chapter as apolitical as possible (at least until the conclusion), since Adams's reasoning was itself mostly apolitical. He gained a lot of support from the Trump wing and a lot of hate from the Clinton wing (and the anti-Trump wing on the right), but if you follow his blog or read his recent book *Win Bigly* (on persuasion in the era of Trump), you can see he finds both the pro- and anti-Trump crowds fundamentally deceiving themselves, while his own (quite progressive) views are ig-nored in favor of merely treating him as a pro-Trumpist by all sides.

But, enough on that background. If you want the full story, either go back and read the archives on Adams's blog, or read *Win Bigly,* which is a good summary of his thought process and reasoning on Trump as a "Master Persuader."

From Derren Brown to Socrates

Since this chapter is in a book on Popular Culture and Philosophy, I need to tie it to philosophy somehow. Luckily, I already had, soon after the election. Rather than give in to cognitive dissonance and try to explain away why I was really right and Trump had really lost—something many on the anti-Trump sides did and still do (and which Adams uses as a good example of how cognitive dissonance works), I had to re-evaluate my own reasoning to see why I was wrong and Adams was correct (or, at least, more correct than I was). I have a PhD in Rhetoric (the art of persuasion) after all. Adams's only stated qualifications came from a hypnosis class he took and a general life-long interest in persuasion.

This served as my first hint at where to go. Adams constantly touts his study of hypnosis as the main reason he sees Trump as a "Master Persuader." In *Win Bigly*, he discusses his hypnosis studies in some detail, but still glosses over most of it, merely stating that studying hypnosis gives him insight into how to persuasion works.

Well, this move made me think of the brilliant British magician/hypnotist/mentalist Derren Brown. In his book, *Tricks of the Mind*, he discusses his experiences with hypnosis, especially as a famous hypnotist himself. He concludes, surprisingly, that hypnosis doesn't really exist, despite some famous examples of him hypnotizing people. He believes hypnosis really just comes from a dominant personality asserting itself on a less dominant one, essentially persuading the other person to behave a certain way or believe a certain thing. The hypnotic state comes more from someone assuming a passive, submissive role (even if they don't realize it) rather than any special hypnotic state of mind.

While Adams does seem to think there is a true hypnotic state, much of what he says about hypnosis fits Brown's ideas: certain people don't make good candidates, the person must be willing to undergo the process, and the hypnotist has to project utter confidence and authority.

So, how did this line of reasoning get me to Socrates? Through Gorgias, an ancient Greek Sophist who dueled (verbally) with Socrates, of course! My mind went from the idea of "hypnosis as persuasion" to "persuasion as magic" that comes from Gorgias. The Sophist Gorgias gave a speech ("The Encomium of Helen"—the title refers to Helen of Troy) where he argued that persuasive words were like magic or powerful drugs, that they could steal someone's free will and cause them to behave in ways they normally wouldn't—and they couldn't be blamed for their behavior because the power of persuasion compelled them to act that way.

Sophistic Sophists who Sophistically Sophistize

So, who was Gorgias? A Sophist, as stated above. Who were the Sophists and how did they relate to Socrates? Well, basically all our modern ideas about rhetoric and persuasion fall into either a Socratic or Sophistic camp. You might be familiar with the term "sophistry," but if not, the Oxford English Dictionary defines it as the "employment of arguments which are intentionally deceptive." We get that term from the Sophists, though it's a bit unfair and mostly due to how Plato portrays them in his Socratic dialogues.

The Sophists—the term itself comes from the Greek word for wisdom; compare how "philosopher" comes from "love" (philo) and "wisdom" (soph) to mean "lover of wisdom"—were traveling teachers in ancient Greece who taught people how to speak and argue well in exchange for money. Basically traveling tutors, they were very popular in city-states such as Athens, because in order to fully participate in society as a citizen, you needed to know how to speak well in public and persuade others, since all citizens (at least in theory) debated about and voted on all issues. The Sophists would travel to an area, give speeches to show off their skill, and then take on paying students.

The main Socratic criticism of them came from the claim that they merely taught outward forms of persuasion, with little care about the underlying truth. A common phrase used to describe them went something like "They make the weaker argument seem the stronger." One ancient play (that calls Socrates a Sophist, despite his opposition to them in Plato's dialogues), *The Clouds*, deals with a son whose Sophistic studies ruins him morally, features a scene where personifications of the Weaker Argument (incorrect) debates the Stronger Argument (the correct) and the Weaker Argument wins through the use of persuasive moves that were clearly logically invalid and ethically questionable—yet were still creatively effective.

In Plato's dialogue *The Sophist*, a character named The Eleatic Stranger spends much of the dialogue trying to define Sophistry, and finally comes up with a somewhat complicated definition; the gist of it is that Sophistry imitates real life but is hollow, empty, insincere, and uninformed. In the *Gorgias*, Gorgias himself admits this, somewhat.

Now, it's hard to say how much of what the character "Gorgias" in the *Gorgias* resembles the actual Gorgias (try not to get lost in all the Gorgias-ing here), but when compared with the fragments of writing we do have from and about Gorgias in other sources, it appears that Plato at least tried to be fair. In the dialogue, Socrates confronts Gorgias and two of his disciples, Polus and Calicles.

Socrates questions Gorgias about rhetoric, and Gorgias admits rhetoric could be used for immoral ends, though he defends rhetoric by likening it to wrestling; sure, someone could learn wrestling so he could go beat up other people more effectively, but that's not the teacher's fault. If a student of Gorgias uses rhetoric for unethical or immoral ends, the teacher shouldn't be blamed. Gorgias hopes his students would be ethical and moral, but it is not something he teaches. He just teaches persuasion.

Socrates argues that studying rhetoric seems unnecessary, because if you are an expert in something, you should already be persuasive about that subject. Gorgias makes the bold claim that he could win a debate with a doctor, despite knowing nothing about medicine. (And now we start getting closer to Adams's Master Persuader hypothesis, that we live in a world where facts don't really matter, all that matters is persuasive power.)

Socrates declares this means rhetoric makes you persuasive to ignorant audiences. (Adams argues that we're all basically ignorant on most issues, so persuasive ability matters more than knowledge.) Rhetoric thus functions like cosmetics that makes a sickly person look well, instead of exercise that makes a person healthy, or like "cookery" that makes unhealthy food attractive vs. actually making healthy, free-range, organic, gluten-free, paleo-friendly meals (okay—Socrates make not have used any of the qualifiers between "healthy" and "meals").

Of course, Gorgias's hope that his students would still behave ethically and morally with their persuasive power seem somewhat dashed when his disciple Polus interjects. According to Polus, rhetoric is awesome because it gives you the power to become a tyrant. With enough persuasive ability, you can rule over people and get them to follow your will.

In the end, Socrates argues that rhetoric, the study of persuasion, is bankrupt in several senses. It has no real subject matter, since the topics must always come from some other area. It preys on the ignorant by dazzling them with grand eloquence while teaching them nothing, and its practitioners often misuse it to gain power. Rhetoricians tell people what they want to hear, rather than what they need to hear, and this corrupts both the audience and the persuader. (Compare this with Scott Adams's claim that the most persuasive move is to play on the fears of an audience, regardless of whether those fears have any real basis.)

In a later dialogue, the *Phaedrus*, Socrates takes a slightly more positive view of rhetoric. While still feeling people too easily and too often misuse it to flatter others and tell them what they want to hear, a more noble version of rhetoric is possible. If used to enlighten others and improve the soul, persuasive techniques serve a useful and important function. The true rhetorician will study people and learn not just how to persuade them, but what they need to become better, improving their souls and enriching their lives.

And, while this is a somewhat simplistic binary, these two versions of rhetoric, the Sophistic (where only persuasive ability matters) and the Socratic (where the moral and ethical improvement of the audience matters most) has dominated and controlled discussion of rhetoric and persuasion since those times (at least in Western culture). When you hear people complain about "mere rhetoric" or declare "let's cut through all the rhetoric," they implicitly refer to the idea of rhetoric as sophistry—that persuasion consists of verbal tricks, clever writing, or other obfuscations of the actual truth. However, the basic academic requirement at pretty much every college or university in Western civilization of a basic writing class (usually with a focus on persuasive writing) is something of an artifact from the Socratic ideal, the idea that good people need to learn persuasion because otherwise only evil people will learn effective persuasion and thus corrupt society.

Theorists of rhetoric—from Aristotle to Cicero to St. Augustine, from Thomas Wilson to Thomas Hobbes to Hugh Blair, from Richard Weaver to Kenneth Burke to Wayne Booth—have all struggled with this dichotomy (don't worry if you don't recognize those names—consider them good names to Google if you want to learn more). St. Augustine, after converting to Christianity, briefly toyed with abandoning the pagan (and thus likely corrupt) arts of rhetoric he had learned as a youth, but he ultimately decided to use rhetoric to help spread the truth of Christ's work, so he developed a type of rhetoric for sermons (known as homiletics).

Thomas Hobbes preferred a short, simple, direct style rather than using the florid, elaborate language favored by many others. Both operated somewhat Socratically, using principles of persuasion to argue for ideas they felt would improve people and society, rather than merely for show or pleasure. However, at the same time, many manuals of rhetoric all through the ages basically taught Sophistic principles (while paying some lip service to Socratic ideals) of florid eloquence and the masterful use of tropes and figures to move and delight audiences, regardless of subject matter.

Okay, Okay—What about Trump and Scott Adams?

I mentioned Adams in a few remarks above, mostly to make sure we didn't forget what this chapter is really about. So, where does Trump and Adams's "Master Persuader" hypothesis fit?

For those knowledgeable about the Sophists, it might seem that Trump doesn't fit. Regardless of whether you support Trump or not, his extemporaneous speech and social media postings don't fit the eloquent phrasings and obsession with style that the Sophists had. However, the Sophists used that style because eloquent speeches with well-constructed sentences and phrases proved persuasive to ancient Greek audiences.

Today, that kind of eloquence is only persuasive to certain audiences. Trump's brand of "eloquence" (if we can call it that) seems fairly persuasive to a very different audience. Often those who support Trump actually like his style, claiming it makes Trump seem down to earth, plain spoken, normal, and otherwise in touch with the common folk.

You don't have to persuade everyone, just enough people. Aristotle (the student of Plato, who studied under and wrote about Socrates) defined rhetoric as the art of finding the available means of persuasion in a given instance. For some situations and audiences, flowery eloquence and grand styles work. In others, plain speech and direct styles work. For Trump, doing whatever it was he did worked to win the Electoral College.

Scott Adams's main contention is that humans are not rational beings. He uses the term "moist robots" for humans, meaning that we basically are biologically programmed to act irrationally, but that someone with the right persuasive skill set can reprogram people, re-wiring them to change beliefs and behaviors. He's using scientific terminology, but Adams is making the same argument as Gorgias: the right set of words—a programming code or a magic spell—can re-wire a person, robbing them of free will.

In *Win Bigly*, Adams cites several scientific studies, from psychology to neuroscience, to make his case, and he seems to be mostly right. As Adams often states, we like to think we're rational, but we very rarely are. This idea bothered Socrates, because he felt the Sophists took advantage of our irrational natures. Socrates wanted to use rhetoric to help humans become more rational, whereas the Sophists basically decided to "go with it," embrace irrationality if that's what it took to "win" the argument. Adams, likewise, isn't bothered by our irrational ways because he feels that's just how we are and we need to learn to live with it.

That's why Adams isn't a Trump shill, despite what those on the alt-right, the anti-Trump right, or the progressive left might think. Attacking or ignoring Adams as a Trump shill just confirms his idea that confirmation bias is a key feature of the operating system. Trump found (whether by accident or design) something that worked, an available means of persuasion (as Aristotle might put it). Scott Adams identified these means and labeled them. Arguing for his hypothesis, he ultimately proved more correct than most political pundits, observers, and other apparent experts.

Adams likes to claim Trump plays "3D" persuasion, whereas most of us think of persuasion in two dimensions, thereby defying the predictions of pundits opposed to him. I personally am not sure whether this 3D persuasive ability is completely intentional on Trump's part, or whether Adams suffers from confirmation bias towards his own "Master Persuader" hypothesis, but the fact is Trump won. Rather than write off Adams as a pro-Trump troll or otherwise rich straight white guy who supported the rich straight white guy for President, I think it best that both supporters and opponents of Trump take a better look at what really happened.

Does this mean that Scott Adams himself is a Sophist? Here's where things get somewhat odd. Adams seems to have a Sophistic view of rhetoric, where all that matters is the tropes, figures, and moves you make when attempting persuasion. And yet, Adams wrote the following in a March 27th 2011 blog post:

> . . . the goal of my writing is to be interesting and nothing else. I'm not trying to change anyone's opinion, largely because I don't believe humans can be influenced by exposure to better arguments, even if I had some. But I do think people benefit by exposure to ideas that are *different* from whatever they are hearing, even when the ideas are *worse*. That's my niche: something different.

This actually shares (somewhat) in the Socratic ideal that people can and should use rhetoric to improve the souls of their audience. Adams isn't trying so much to change the world by persuading people to agree with him. He wants to improve the world by exposing people to arguments and ideas they might otherwise never entertain. Ultimately, I feel Adams is mostly in the Sophistic mode, as he focuses on what rhetorical moves are most persuasive and feels that the right appeals function like programming code (or magic) on human brains. But Adams still borrows some of that Socratic ideal of persuasive techniques, causing people to break out of their mental chains, upgrading their moist robot operating systems.

To deal effectively with Trump, those who oppose him need to see how he won and what he did to win. Those who support Trump should be aware of what Trump did as well, since even Adams likes to point out how Trump supporters often rationalize away their decisions without realizing how persuasion worked on them. Adams may not have all the answers, but he has enough of them. I don't advocate going "full Adams" (on this, or anything, really), but I do advocate for carefully considering his insights on one aspect of Trump's victory.

And, of course, I have been attempting to persuade you, the reader, that Adams actually does have some of the answers. Do I agree with Adams? That depends on what you mean by "agree"—and I'm not sophistically dodging the question. I agree with Adams that too often people let their cognitive dissonance and confirmation biases overcome their ability to rationally consider ideas. I agree that far too often, a crafty politician (or boss or whatever) can use rhetorically powerful yet irrational arguments to win the day. Yet, at the same time, I'm not ready to give up the Socratic ideal that people can think rationally, and that it is possible to overcome your cognitive biases if you try hard enough. And that's what this chapter is really about—I want those who write Adams off as a far-right, pro-Trump troll to understand what Adams is really doing, learning what they can from his insights. And, I hope that those who see Adams as a hero of the Trump movement realize what's really going on and perhaps find themselves more aware of how persuasion (whether from Trump, Adams, me, or anyone else) attempts to cast a spell on them/rewrite their programming.

Adams may have abandoned the idea of rational discourse that overcomes cognitive biases; I'm hoping to move the conversation in a more rational direction (although I admit Adams has a bigger audience and more engaging writing style, so from a Sophistic standpoint, he's way ahead).

2
Persuade Me Once, Shame on You . . .

RICHARD GREENE

In *Win Bigly: Persuasion in a World Where Facts Don't Matter* Scott Adams argues that Donald Trump is what he calls a "Master Persuader" (the rarest of persuaders, whose peers include the likes of Steve Jobs and Warren Buffett) who has "weapons-grade persuasion skills."

Adams himself is a self-proclaimed "commercial-grade" persuader who has thought and written extensively on the topic, and asserts he has the ability to raise his persuasion powers to weapons-grade when called upon to do so. If Adams is right about this, then a lot of us have quite a bit of rethinking to do on the question of whether Trump is masterful at anything. To at least a large segment of the world population, Trump is a kind of buffoon, or a caricature of a politician. Of course, if Adams is in fact a commercial-grade persuader (again with weapons-grade persuasion skills at his disposal), he should have no trouble convincing even the most hardened skeptic of the truth of his claims. We'll see.

Believe Me Folks, The Following Argument Is Not Good, That Much I Can Tell You!

One argument in favor of the view that Trump is a Master Persuader lies in the fact that he won the election. Trump did convince enough people to vote for him, such that he received more than enough electoral college votes to secure victory. It's fair to say that in an election, precisely what candidates are doing is attempting to persuade people to vote for them, and that's exactly what Trump did.

This is not an argument offered by Adams, and with good reason. There are a number of problems with this argument. Most importantly, to adopt this view would be to hold that anyone who won an election (or at least a significant election) would count as a Master Persuader. Related to this is the fact that a lot of factors go into determining who wins an election, many of which have little to do with the actions of the candidates involved. For example, the political and economic climate at the time often play a huge role. After the Watergate scandal, there was virtually no hope that any Republican candidate would win the 1976 Presidential Election. Few, I believe, hold the view that Jimmy Carter was a Master Persuader. Many people hold him in extremely high esteem (especially for his principles and humanitarian work), but even his most ardent supporters are loath to praise his persuasion skills.

Another related factor is the fact that it's not just the candidates themselves, in an election, who are doing the persuading. There are literally hundreds of surrogates out speaking on behalf of the candidates at nearly all times. They are attempting to persuade voters to vote for their candidate of choice on cable news programs, at rallies, at $1,500 a plate dinners, and at scores of other events. In addition to the army of surrogates, there are people not officially affiliated with the campaigns also doing a lot of persuading. Celebrities are making their endorsements, and people in bars are attempting to convince their friends whom to vote for. This list goes on and on.

A second worry about this argument is that it waters down the concept of "Master Persuader." It's almost never a good idea to define a concept in terms of success related to the goals of that concept. For example, we don't want to define a "good quarterback" as one who almost always wins football games, even though winning football games is the sort of thing that good quarterbacks generally or routinely do. Famous Trump supporter Tom Brady is a good quarterback and he routinely wins games, but he is not a good quarterback merely because he routinely wins games. He's a good quarterback because he has the requisite skills (reads defenses well, retains his composure while under pressure, throws the football accurately, manages the clock well, and so forth).

By contrast, Archie Manning was also considered a great quarterback. He was dynamic, could make plays, had a great arm, etc., but spent his entire career on really bad teams. We don't want to define quarterback greatness, purely in terms of success, and the same applies to presidential candidates. Further there are many marginal quarterbacks who almost always win games because other players on their teams are really good (recall the year the Baltimore Ravens won the Super Bowl with Trent Dilfer as their quarterback). Thus, I think we can dispense with the idea that Trump is a Master Persuader just because he won.

Adams's position that Trump is a Master Persuader, much to his credit, is a more nuanced position, and it relies on a considerably more complex argument than the one just canvassed.

So just what is Adam's argument for the position that Trump is a Master Persuader? It's a two-phase argument where in the first phase he describes the characteristics a Master Persuader must have, arguing further that Trump, indeed, has those characteristics, and in the second phase argues that Trump has somehow changed reality, and that via a different way of viewing reality, it becomes clear that Trump is a Master Persuader. The idea is that only a Master Persuader could do such things, or his doing so constitutes evidence for his being a Master Persuader.

With This Argument, Adams Is Winning Again!

Just what is a Master Persuader? On Adams's view, persuasion is a matter of using tools and techniques to change people's minds. This can occur with or without facts or reason. A Master Persuader (one with weapons-grade persuasion skills) is one who can do this deftly and effectively, and presumably does not make a great deal of persuasive mistakes along the way. In an appendix to *Win Bigly: Persuasion in a World Where Facts Don't Matter*, Adams lists a number of Trump's notable mistakes (for example, Trump University), but none of them appear to be mistakes in an attempt to persuade.

Apparently, on Adams's account, the way to spot a Master Persuader is to find someone who has done some serious persuading and see if they do the things that master persuaders do. So, what are those things? Adams details a number of things that Master Persuaders do.

Master Persuaders who are attempting to make a deal start with big demands and then move back to the middle. He cites Trump's campaign promises pertaining to the mass deportation of immigrants as an example of this. On the campaign trail Trump repeatedly promised to "round up" illegals and send them home (making similar claims about keeping out Muslims). The idea here is that getting what you want is often a matter of negotiation. A nuanced view will seem more reasonable and facilitate getting one what you want.

The worry about applying this tactic to Trump is that it is not at all clear that this is what he was intending to do. At the time this is being written, Trump has not nuanced his position on illegal immigrants, nor offered anything of a more reasonable nature. And for that matter, he initially attempted to enact his extreme-sounding ban on Muslims entering the country only to have the courts thwart his efforts. Further, while it seems right to say that this is a strategy that Master Persuaders employ, it hardly counts as evidence that someone is a Master Persuader, as it is a strategy that virtually everyone employs when they find themselves negotiating. My twelve-year-old son employs this strategy whenever he wants to stay out with his friends later than we agreed upon. His opening salvo is always "Can I have two more hours?" knowing full well that I'll come back with "How about one?"

To be sure, Adams is not arguing that anyone who does something that a Master Persuader does is herself a Master Persuader. Nor is he arguing that only Master Persuaders do these things. Rather, his position appears to be that anyone who does most or all of the things on his list must be a Master Persuader. (Note that he never actually says this, but if this is not his position, it's not at all clear why he's arguing in this way. Perhaps he's attempting to be a Master Persuader by just saying "Trump" and "Master Persuader" a lot in the same sentences, without regard for the facts, in hopes of getting us to believe that Trump is one.) While I'm inclined to leave "starting with big demands and moving towards the middle" off the list of necessary and sufficient conditions for Master Persuader status, I'm willing to move on to some of the other claims in hopes of definitively settling the question of whether Trump is, in fact, a Master Persuader.

Adams's next claim is that, at times, Master Persuaders can still be persuasive while ignoring facts. In fact, Trump routinely employs a strategy that Adams calls "The Intentional Wrongness Persuasion Play." The idea is that the persuader says something intentionally wrong, but somehow in the direction of something truthful (for example, when he exaggerates a fact). This leads to people thinking about and discussing what was said for considerably longer than they would have, had he said something accurate, which combines with the basic psychological fact that the more time someone spends thinking about something the more important it will seem to that person, and the higher priority they will place on it. Later Adams sums up this point by stating that facts are weaker than fiction.

It's well documented that Trump's relation with facts and the truth is, putting it mildly, a tenuous one at best. The question is whether his playing fast and loose with the facts stems from an understanding of something like The Intentional Wrongness Persuasion Play (or some close variant) or something else entirely. For example, he may just be a serial liar, or he might enjoy the media attention he gets when his lies are discussed (he has been telling public lies, such as lies about Obama not being born in the U.S., since long before he became a presidential candidate).

At this point, however, it's worth noting that Trump isn't obviously intentionally using false statements in accordance with some persuasive strategy, such as the Intentional Wrongness Persuasion Play. It could well be the case that he believes the things he says. For example, I've met people who have a strong inclination to believe anything that they think, as if their thinking it makes it seem reasonable. Perhaps Trump is one of these types. I don't think that he is, but Adams owes an argument that 1. rules out this possibility, and 2. provides good reason to believe that Trump is employing the same strategies that a Master Persuader would employ.

Another strategy that Master Persuaders employ is to create a desire to reciprocate in the person being persuaded. If Trump does things for folks along the campaign trail, then they might feel obligated to reciprocate (Adams says that humans are hard-wired to reciprocate). To the extent that Trump was giving his voters what they wanted (such as a place for their racist "Build the Wall" chant), he was likely playing on their desire to reciprocate.

Adams also points out that Master Persuaders don't apologize too much, and display lots of confidence. Apologizing causes people to remember that you were wrong. Confidence makes folks believe that you're not wrong. Combining this with some of the considerations above, being wrong can be good, as it gets folks talking and thinking, but having their final impression on any matter be that you were wrong, is ultimately bad. Certainly no one would accuse Trump of being a serial apologizer. Whether he was intentionally employing the strategies of creating a desire to reciprocate, exuding confidence, and not apologizing too much is another question. Adams, again, owes us more if he is going to make the case that Trump is a Master persuader, and not just coincidentally doing things that master persuaders do.

Finally, it's not enough to do these things, but you need what Adams calls: a "Talent Stack," that is a strong series of skills. According to his view, Trump's talent stack is impressive. It includes: publicity skills, a good reputation, strategic skills, negotiating skills, skills of persuasion, public speaking skills, a good sense of humor, quickness on his feet, being thick-skinned, being high-energy, having a certain stature, and above average intelligence. In the interest of brevity, I'll not tackle these one by one. Suffice it so say that in some cases the jury is still out with respect to Trump, and in other cases it is clear that he has the talents Adams attributes to him, but it certainly seems true that these could be useful traits to have were one interested in being a Master Persuader.

To this point we've not been given much of an argument that Trump is a Master Persuader. We've seen that he does some of the things that Master Persuaders do (ignores facts when it suits them, doesn't apologize, makes grand claims, exhibits confidence, create a desire to in folks reciprocate, and so forth), but merely doing things that a Master Persuader does is not sufficient to make you a Master Persuader. Paraphrasing Immanuel Kant (who was speaking in another context), it's not enough to do the right thing; you must do the right thing for the right reason.

Further, Adams has not actually supported the claim that Trump has persuaded anyone of anything. If we consider persuasion a matter of getting people to believe something, Trump's consistently low poll numbers tend to indicate that few who didn't already believe the things that he was saying were convinced by him. If we consider persuasion a matter of getting people to behave in certain ways his pretty low voter turnout, as compared with Hillary Clinton, tends to indicate that few who weren't already inclined to vote for him (or vote Republican or vote against Clinton) were persuaded to vote for him. The Electoral College can be a fickle mistress.

We're Going to Make Reality Great Again!

The second phase of Adams's argument that Trump is a Master Persuader is more interesting. Adam's states that "the common worldview, shared by most humans, is that there is one objective reality, and we humans can understand that reality through a rigorous application of facts and reason."

He cites a number of philosophers from Plato to Hume to Kant and beyond to support the idea that reality is not something immediately accessible to us. Hume is quite agnostic on the nature of reality, and Kant postulates two realities (the phenomenal world and the noumenal world) one of which we have access to, and one of which we do not, but Plato actually holds the opposite view that Adams is using him to support. Adams at one point says "the main theme of this book is that humans are not rational." A corollary of this claim is that humans are mistaken when they believe that their rationality will lead them to understand their reality. Plato believes that only our rationality will lead us to an understanding of reality, even if reality is different from what we initially take it to be.

So how does all this philosophical mumbo-jumbo bear on Trump as Master Persuader? Adams's view seems to be that since there is no objective reality, then we're not going to be able to get at objective reality using reason and perceptual skills. He offers the fact that all the so-called experts were wrong about how the election would turn out, and that they were wrong at each stage of the argument about Trump (for example his early remarks about John McCain not being a hero were supposed to be a deal breaker, as were his comments about the Gold Star family members, as was his failure to disavow the KKK, as were his remarks about sexually assaulting women, and so on), as evidence that reality is not what it seems.

His arguments miss the mark somewhat. Just because it's hard to get things right doesn't really mean there is no objective reality. And our predictive successes based on past experience (think of Rick Perry's 2011 predictably quick political demise when he couldn't recall the name of a federal agency he wanted to eliminate), shouldn't necessarily translate to predictive success in future cases, even if there is an objective reality. (See Hume on the Problem of Induction.)

Still, a less clumsy version of Adams's argument presents itself and might run as follows. Since 1. we need to make sense out of the world, and 2. our rational faculties are not up to the task (due to the prevalence of cognitive dissonance, mass hysteria, and confirmation bias), we need to employ filters to do so. Filters don't take us directly to reality, but if they are good, give us better predictions about the future. We have a number of filters available to us, but, according to Adams, the Persuasion Filter is the one that has the most predictive value in this context. It's the one that best explained why Trump was going to win prior to his doing so.

To his credit, Adams's employment of the Persuasion Filter got this right. That said, there is nothing to link Adams's take on Trump (via the Persuasion Filter) and Trump's victory. Given that Trump's victory defied the expectations of many, you would expect that similarly constituted past presidential candidates would have yielded similar results. We've had no shortage of bombastic politicians who play fast and loose with the facts, yet this is the first time someone such as Trump has ascended to the presidency. Of course, the circumstances were not identical. I suspect that going forward we will have plenty of candidates using Trump's exact playbook in hope of achieving the same level of success. I'll predict now that it won't soon work again, but time will tell. At any rate, Adams's line of argumentation does not give us any reason to believe that Trump is a Master Persuader.

3
How I Could Have Made Hillary President

David Ramsay Steele

In his book *Win Bigly: Persuasion in a World Where Facts Don't Matter*, Scott Adams analyzes the formidable persuasion skills of Donald Trump and the comparatively feeble persuasion techniques of the Hillary Clinton campaign of 2016. The book is very funny, full of insights, and well worth reading. For those who haven't read it, what I'm going to talk about here is a tiny sliver of the richly entertaining material in the book, but it does illustrate Adams's approach.

Adams compares what he calls Trump's "linguistic kill shots" with the attempted kill shots of the Hillary campaign, and he compares Trump's slogan, "Make America Great Again" with the numerous easily forgettable slogans considered or actually employed by the Hillary campaign.

Here are the more powerful of Trump's linguistic kill shots:

- **Low-energy Jeb**
- **Crooked Hillary**
- **Lyin' Ted**
- **Lil' Marco**
- **Pocahontas**

Scott Adams analyzes these in detail to show exactly why they're so effective. They all appeal to the visual and they all plan for "confirmation bias." Probably the best of them is "Low-energy Jeb." The very day this nickname came out of Trump's mouth, Scott Adams blogged that Jeb! was finished, as indeed he was, though no other commentator saw what had just happened. Recall that Jeb Bush had a war chest of many millions and spent far more than Trump. He was a natural for traditional Republican voters and for the fabled "Republican establishment," as yet another dynastic Bush but a more likeable personality than the preceding two Bushes.

Even after Trump had released his kill shot into what we can call the *rhetorosphere*, most seasoned pundits were still naming "Jeb!" as the most likely nominee. Yet, Trump had given Jeb Bush what Adams calls his "forever name," and it was henceforth to be altogether impossible for anyone to see Jeb! or think about him without instantly thinking *low-energy*. His presidential ambition had been killed stone dead, his millions of dollars nullified, not just for that electoral cycle but for all time, in about half a second, "in front of your eyes," by the Master Persuader, Donald Trump.

Adams offers similar analyses for the other nicknames. "Pocahontas" was the name given to Elizabeth Warren, one of the leading Democratic Party politicians and a likely future Democratic presidential candidate. Warren, a blue-eyed blonde, had claimed to be of Native American, specifically Cherokee, ancestry and had gotten an academic job at Harvard after representing herself as a "minority." The Cherokee Nation, which has a database of everyone they have been able to find with Cherokee ancestry, has repeatedly protested against Warren's claim. Warren also once contributed a "Native American" recipe to a book of supposedly Native American recipes called . . . wait for it . . . *Pow Wow Chow*. It turns out that Warren is not Native American, the recipe was not Native American but French, and the recipe itself was plagiarized from another source.

A look at this book on Amazon shows that Warren is in even deeper trouble. The subtitle of *Pow Wow Chow* is *A Col-*

lection of Recipes from Families of the Five Civilized Tribes, and the book is published by Five Civilized Tribes Museum. This blatantly insinuates that the Apache didn't routinely solve quadratics or use trig to calculate the circumference of the Earth, and that is indisputably the filthiest kind of racism.

I would be irresponsible if I didn't point out that this kill shot illustrates Donald Trump's disgraceful carelessness with facts. The Cherokee belong to the Iroquoian group, whereas the historical Pocahontas belonged to an Algonquian-speaking tribe. How low have we sunk when our president can tell such appalling lies?

Everyone could see that Trump's nicknames were effective, and so the Hillary campaign burned the midnight oil to discover an effective nickname for Trump himself. They tried three in succession:

- **Donald Duck**

- **Dangerous Donald**

- **Drumpf**

"Donald Duck" is obviously the sort of thing a committee would come up with. "Duck" tries to make the point that Trump was "ducking" various issues and various criticisms, including releasing his tax returns. But of course, associating Trump with a beloved if distinctly ridiculous cartoon character doesn't mesh well with the idea that Trump is a fearful Hitler-like menace.

"Dangerous Donald" doesn't really work, especially because a large portion of the electorate positively wanted someone "dangerous," someone who would go to Washington and break things.

"Drumpf" is the real surname of Trump's Austrian immigrant ancestor, a perfectly respectable German name which isn't so congenial to Americans, so it was changed to "Trump." This idea that having a non-Anglo-Saxon name in your family tree is a dirty little secret is not a winner, for several obvious reasons.

As everyone knows, Trump's election slogan was "Make America Great Again." This is a brilliant slogan which can hardly be faulted. Adams lists its strong points (*Win Bigly*, pp. 155–56).

As against this, the Hillary campaign considered eighty-five slogans (yes, 85!, according to Scott Adams, p. 157, citing the *New York Times*) and eventually ended up with "Stronger Together." Here are the ones which were actually tried out.

- **Love Trumps Hate**
- **I'm with Her**
- **I'm ready for Hillary**
- **Fighting for Us**
- **Breaking Down Barriers**
- **Stronger Together**

These all have the flavor of mediocrity and ineffectiveness that comes out of committees, and especially committees of bigoted leftists. "Love Trumps Hate" literally begins with "Love Trump," and as Scott Adams points out, people's attentiveness declines steeply, so they often pay more attention to the beginning than to the end of a sentence.

"I'm with Her" and "I'm Ready for Hillary" both have a patronizing tone, as though you can prove yourself by being open to a female candidate, just because she's female; that kind of thing is off-putting to some voters. And as Bill Maher pointed out, "Ready for Hillary" evokes the resignation of being "ready" for that uncomfortable tetanus shot from that possibly sadistic nurse.

"Fighting for Us" makes you wonder who the "Us" really is. During World War II, George Orwell pointed out how a British working man might interpret the government poster that said: "*Your* Courage, *Your* Cheerfulness, *Your* Resolution, will bring *Us* Victory" (the first three sets of italics in the original, the fourth definitely not!).

"Breaking Down Barriers" has good rhythm but an uncertain appeal because most people feel strongly that they really want some barriers between them and some kinds of other people.

"Stronger Together" was the final throw, and it came just as voters could hardly ignore the fact that violence was coming from the left. Some of Hillary supporters were bullies, and bullies are always stronger together. The news was already out that the "violence at Trump's rallies" was deliberately engineered by paid agents of the DNC.

Scott Adams Doesn't Give His Alternatives!

Although Scott does an excellent job of identifying the strengths of Trump's slogan and nicknames for opponents, and the weaknesses of Hillary's, he doesn't come up with his own, better proposals for Hillary.

This is a bit of a disappointment, and a surprise, as he emphasizes that it's all a matter of conscious technique, not instinct.

And so, I decided to cook up my own suggestions. Here goes!

My proposal for the nickname Hillary should have given Trump is:

- **The Don**

Here's how this works. Before Trump announced for president, he was often called "The Donald," a phrase which usually went along with either patronizing amusement or mild and grudging admiration. Use of "The Donald" died out, presumably because the US population was mobilizing into two great camps, one of which viewed Trump as a satanic monster, the other of which saw him as the nation's redeemer, and neither of these would perceive "The Donald" as entirely apt.

My plan would be for Hillary supporters to refer to him several times as "The Don," and just occasionally, for those who might be a bit slow on the uptake, "The Godfather" (or variations like "The Godfather of Greed"). Hillary would then take up "The Don," as an already established nickname for Trump.

Trump has many of the popular attributes of the Mafia boss: a commanding presence and a weakness for vulgar display (his golden toilets). All the points actually made against Trump's character by Clinton could have been given a slightly different coloration. Thus, when making the allegation (which the Hillary campaign did) that Trump had stiffed some of his sub-contractors, this would be described as "making them an offer they couldn't refuse." You could throw in a reference to one of Trump's business dealings with someone who has since passed on, and add the jocular remark, "He now sleeps with the fishes." When complaining about the fact that Trump wouldn't release his tax returns, this could be framed as "the Trump Family [Family, get it?] has sworn the oath of *Omertà* never to reveal their sources of income."

But aren't mafiosi supposed to be Italian? Yes, but now they're often Russian too. Hillary's campaign promoted the story that Trump had "colluded with the Russians." This appears to have been a pure fabrication, simply made up by the Hillary campaign (no one has ever faulted Hillary for being over-scrupulous or excessively candid) but it would have been so much more believable if associated with the Russian mafia.

It's a self-evident truth that every Russian has "ties to Vladimir Putin," and this can always be asserted of any Russian without fear of rebuttal. Similarly, it's a self-evident truism that every Russian businessman has "ties to the Russian mob." It would have been a simple matter to dig up every occasion when Trump did business with a Russian, call that Russian an "oligarch" (who could deny it?), and declare that this Russian oligarch had ties to organized crime (or deny that?). In this way, it would have become impossible for voters not to think of Trump's business activities as steeped in criminality.

Now, what about a campaign slogan for Hillary? This is quite difficult, because of the fact that Hillary had spent four of the previous eight years as Secretary of State within the Obama administration. She could not therefore put any emphasis on "change," and it would be hard to imply anything radically new. But anything that looked like a defense of the last eight years could only run the risk of implying that "the status quo is fine and we just want to keep things the way they are." This is a disadvantageous position to be in.

A slogan that goes negative and tries to focus on the evil of Trump is liable to boomerang—remember that meeting of Democrats, where a speaker referred to Hillary using the word "honest," and the entire room spontaneously erupted into laughter?

As Scott Adams hilariously points out (p. 159), a rather different kind of boomerang was a major feature of the campaign. One of Trump's problems, as a former reality TV host, was to get voters to take him seriously as a real president. Hillary continually urged voters to "imagine" Trump as president, and thus provided Trump with exactly what he needed. He needed people to imagine him as president, and Hillary did an excellent job of helping voters to do just that.

The Hillary campaign slogan has to have the following qualities:

- **It mustn't directly mention the rival product.**

- **It mustn't be easily interpreted as merely a response to Trump's slogan or campaign.**

- **It can't, unfortunately, make a bold plea for change.**

- **It can't, unfortunately, make a bold claim for Hillary's trustworthiness or other personal virtues.**

- **It must have rhythm.**

- **It mustn't allow the interpretation that some special interest will be benefited.**

- **It must take the high ground.**

So here's my proposal:

- **A Win-Win for America**

This slogan would occasionally follow the words "Hillary Rodham Clinton." (It's bad luck that "HRC" doesn't trip off the tongue like "LBJ" or even "JFK." There is no other memorable version comparable with "Doubleya." "HRC" might evoke "hardcore," but we probably don't want to go there.)

The slogan is positive and inclusively patriotic. It therefore crowds out the undesirable thought that Hillary appeals chiefly to welfare recipients, criminal aliens, and billionaire hedge-fund managers. "For America" takes the high ground and crowds out the thought that Hillary's election would be a win for Hillary, an undesirable thought because Hillary might be considered a loser, and also because we don't want voters thinking about any personal advantage Hillary might reap.

The term "Win-Win" has several functions. Literally it refers to a situation where we win, whichever of two alternate possibilities occurs. There would have to be a story about this, ready for those times when Hillary or her henchmen were directly asked about the meaning. But that's unimportant. We could even come up with a dozen different stories and get people arguing about which one was true. (Someone might suggest that it referred to the two Clintons in the White House again, and we might let that kick around for forty-eight hours before squashing it.) Really the term is simply a repetition of the positive word "win," and gives the slogan distinctiveness and rhythm.

It also has something which Scott Adams has talked about on a number of occasions: he has pointed out how President Trump utilizes the tried and tested marketing ploy of putting slightly "wrong" formulations into his tweets to enhance their effectiveness. A slightly doubtful formulation or a feeling that something is not quite conventionally correct helps a phrase to lodge in the memory. "Win-Win" therefore gains something from the fact that what it means is slightly obscure and off-key, while its emotional associations are entirely positive.

So there we are, Trump is *The Don* and Hillary's slogan is *A Win-Win for America*. This would have been enough to give her the electoral college, though it wouldn't have hurt to have also done a bit more campaigning in Michigan and Wisconsin.

Hillary threw tens of millions of dollars at various "consultants" who were out of their depth and out of touch with public feeling. As I've just proved, I could have gotten Hillary elected by a few commonsense marketing touches. Given my unpretentious proletarian origins and unimpressive net worth, I would have done it for, say, half a million dollars. That would have been a terrific deal for Hillary, and would have enabled me to pay off a good chunk of my debts.

But, I can already hear you saying, you'd be enabling this disgusting warmonger, purveyor of PC bigotry, and criminal sociopath to take power. Could you really live with yourself?

Yes, I have to admit, I would feel bad about that. So, make it a round million.[1]

---

[1] With a few slight differences, this chapter was posted on the London Libertarian blog (http://blog.la-articles.org.uk) on 22nd February 2018.

II

Comic-Strip Kafka

4
Scoundrels, the Lot of Us

JOHN V. KARAVITIS

In 2016, four out of five Americans worked in the service sector. I believe that this goes a long way toward explaining the popularity of *Dilbert*, the American comic strip created by Scott Adams.

Dilbert uses satire to criticize a work environment that many Americans experience daily. Readers relate to what the characters experience and say about America's "white-collar" workplace and the bizarre and oftentimes counter-productive attitudes, behaviors, and thoughts of both managers and employees.

Working in an office can be very stressful. For those of us who struggle in this world, we don't just "work in an office." We find ourselves constantly dealing with people whom we didn't choose to spend an entire day with, day after day, for an indeterminate future. We spend our workdays trying to solve problems while at the same time dealing with office politics and the "crazy" of everyone else. (It's always everyone else who's crazy, of course.) And although it may not seem so at first glance, a satirical comic strip like *Dilbert*—because it deals with people and life—has plenty of *philosophy* lurking in the background.

I Said; You Said; But What We *Really* Meant . . .

The first thing you notice in a *Dilbert* comic strip is its format. Typically, there are three separate drawings, or "panels," that present a quick verbal exchange either between a manager and an employee, or between employees. A statement is made in each panel, and the result is that the reader experiences a verbal exchange that is satirical in nature.

But that's a simplistic look at the surface. If you look more deeply into the verbal exchange, you will realize that a pattern exists. The first panel has a statement that expresses a position. The second panel has a statement that in some sense counters this position, either by rejecting it outright or by pointing out an exception to it. The second panel is a reaction to the first panel. The third panel resolves the first two panels, bringing them into harmony by showing that they are both consequences of a greater truth.

This careful analysis may seem pedantic for something as simple as a satirical comic strip. But, given the way I've dissected the panels, and established the relationship among them, it's clear that there is an overall structure to *Dilbert*.

Let's call the first panel the "thesis." The second panel is counter to the first panel, so let's call that panel the "antithesis." Since the third panel takes both preceding panels and explains any apparent contradiction, let's call the third panel the "synthesis." This synthesis of the thesis and the antithesis is itself a new idea that reveals a deeper truth about the world. It does this by acknowledging and integrating both the thesis and the antithesis. If you really want to get philosophical about it, the flow of the statements made in the three panels reveals itself to be a *Hegelian dialectic*.

Georg Wilhelm Friedrich Hegel (1770–1831) was a German philosopher who sought to create a complete system of philosophy. The goal of this system was to provide an objective view of reality. One of the ideas within Hegel's philosophy was that the world was continually and inexorably moving toward what he termed "absolute truth." Hegel believed that, at any given point in time, the world had within it the seeds of its own destruction. This destruction would lead to a new, better world.

In fact, all of history could be looked at as the story of the world moving toward a final, absolute truth—a best of all possible worlds. The world as it is *now* represents a thesis. The seeds of the world's destruction—which are the contradictions that are a part of the world as it is now—form the antithesis. The consensus that results from the interaction between the two is a synthesis—a new world that replaces the old.

Adams probably didn't plan this at the outset. I mean, the dialectic really is a common way that people talk about things, isn't it? Someone states a position about a topic. Someone else either counters this position or highlights an exception to it. And then, a new idea is eventually arrived at that brings the two opposing positions into harmony. This new idea leads us to a deeper appreciation of how the world works. You see? There *is* philosophy in *Dilbert*! You just have to dig a little to find it.

It's the dialectic that makes philosophy a search for the truth. Adams may have inadvertently turned millions of Americans into cubicle-dwelling, deskbound philosophers! But for now, we've really only just scratched the surface of the typical *Dilbert* comic strip. Can we dig deeper? Surely the structure supports something more . . . philosophical!

Don't Make Me Think! I Just Want to Laugh!

You may be wondering if there's really any point to what I've just said, and there is. *Dilbert*'s structure supports the message presented in the verbal exchanges between the characters. When you read a *Dilbert* comic strip, you're being shown a facet of the white-collar workplace that seems confusing, contradictory, or even nonsensical. Managers are shown as being incompetent or oblivious, and fellow employees as difficult or just plain crazy. Reading *Dilbert* can make you feel as if you're the only person who can see the proverbial train racing toward you and everyone else, and you can't seem to warn anyone about it. (Assuming that you can first get the proper forms filled out, in triplicate; reviewed; and approved in time!)

I referred to *Dilbert* as a "satirical comic strip." And it certainly is. Satire is criticism that uses wit, humor, or exaggeration to expose people's foibles, vices, or lack of good judgment in a specific context. We know that Adams is criticizing the absurdity of the white-collar workplace, but there's something deeper—something *philosophical*—here. *Dilbert* comic strips are utilizing a literary device called *irony*.

The root of the word irony comes from the ancient Greek *eirôn*, "dissembling scoundrel," who was a character in ancient Greek comedies. The *eirôn*'s goal was to bring down another character who had bragged about his abilities, and the *eirôn* did this by trivializing his own. Irony is indirect communication which conveys a truth about a situation subtly through a contradiction: the discrepancy between what is expected and what eventually occurs. So, when we say that someone is being ironic, we understand that he is saying one thing, yet means another. This contradiction is never explicitly stated. It can't and still be irony. In a sense, understanding irony requires you to be both inside of a situation and outside of it at the same time. The contradiction must be inferred by the reader or listener, so context is important in irony.

Although there are many forms of irony, they all fall within three basic types: verbal, situational, and dramatic. When used verbally, irony gives the writer or speaker tools such as sarcasm, understatement, and hyperbole. All of these tools are used in *Dilbert*. As I was thinking about how irony is communicated, I found myself wondering whether there had ever been a wordless *Dilbert* comic strip! Is such a thing possible? I mean, Japanese *manga* (comic books) are sometimes wordless, as are a number of current American and European comic books. However, I've been told that to date this has never happened in *Dilbert*. (Dilbert.com Help Desk, personal communication, December 28th 2017.)

Would past philosophers have appreciated *Dilbert*? The earliest philosopher to whom we could point would be Socrates (470–399 B.C.E.). Socrates is famous for the way he encouraged people to question the basic assumptions and definitions that they held dear, all the while showing them that they in fact didn't have a clear understanding of what they were talking about!

Talk about being ironic! Socrates used feigned ignorance and persistent questioning to draw his audience to what philosophers call an "aporia"—a logical impasse or contradiction. In this way, Socrates sought to show his audience that those who claimed to know something were in fact those who were the most ignorant—most of all, of their own ignorance! Socrates never gave his audience an answer to the questions discussed in any of his dialogs. But by experiencing critical self-reflection through a Socratic dialog, Socrates's audience would have had the opportunity to take responsibility for their assumptions and try to change them. Since Socrates never resolved the question at hand, his relationship to irony could be understood as neutral. (Although, clearly, he indulged in it.)

Two more recent philosophers had much stronger opinions on the use of irony in the search for truth: Hegel, whom we encountered earlier in this chapter, and Danish philosopher Søren Aabye Kierkegaard (1813–1855). In *Aesthetik* (1835), Hegel was critical of irony and its usefulness. Irony is grounded in ambiguity. There is a surface meaning, along with a hidden meaning which contradicts it. For Hegel, this meant that anyone who relies on irony wasn't taking the world seriously. Not being serious about the world means that people would withdraw from it and embrace vanity. Embracing vanity would mean looking inward, and therefore the individual would not be able to accept objective reality. Irony creates a subjective, not an objective, relationship between a writer or speaker and his audience. Hegel was creating a complete system of philosophy, one that would lead to *objective* reality. For Hegel, irony could not be part of a process by which we could work toward absolute truth. Hegel saw irony in a negative light.

Kierkegaard however saw irony as life-affirming. In his doctoral dissertation, *On the Concept of Irony: With Continual Reference to Socrates* (1841), Kierkegaard saw irony as leading us to passionately relate to revelations about the world, and to eventually take responsibility for what we believe in. It's not enough to just show someone that their assumptions are wrong. He must be willing to take responsibility for them and change them. The possibility of changing for the better makes Kierkegaard's view of irony positive.

So now we've seen that the literary device used in *Dilbert*, irony, comes loaded with philosophical implications. And depending on which philosopher you're talking to, irony can be neutral, negative, or positive. But is that it? Can we call it a day and head for home? Not yet.

First Let's Play . . .

So far we've seen that, surprisingly, *Dilbert* comes packed with a lot of philosophy! First, the comic strip panels have a structure which can be referred to as a Hegelian dialectic. Second, the message that the panels communicate is delivered through the literary device of irony. But before I draw any final conclusions from the philosophy we've uncovered in *Dilbert* (my philosophical hat trick for this chapter, if you will), let's take a well-deserved break around the office water cooler and have a little harmless fun at *Dilbert*'s expense.

There are three sequential panels in a *Dilbert* strip, each containing a statement. We can sequentially label the panels "Thesis, Antithesis, and Synthesis." The structure is compact, and the message contained within it requires us to look past the surface meaning to a hidden, perhaps contradictory, meaning. Decoding the comic strip's message depends on context, so the reader has to use his experience and intuition to understand the irony and to arrive at the truth within it. If you take a step back and think about it, this setup should sound quite familiar. When thinking about the structure of *Dilbert*, I found myself thinking about another art form. Can you think of any other work of art which resembles this? A compact, three-part structure, with a hidden meaning, and you'll want to be very careful about the number of syllables.

Dilbert comic strips are a visual and textual form of haiku.

A haiku is a form of Japanese poetry, and most of us were exposed to it in grammar school. Haikus have compact structures: three short lines, with each line having a fixed number of syllables. A haiku communicates its message by contrasting two apparently opposite images or ideas. It uses a "cutting word" (in Japanese, *kireji*), whose purpose is to show how the two opposing ideas relate to each other. Sounds familiar, doesn't it? I'm pretty sure that Adams didn't have this in mind for *Dilbert*. Nevertheless, it shows that similar ways of parsing reality exist in both the West and the East.

In fact, when it comes to messages and hidden meanings, saying one thing and meaning another appears to have existed throughout the history of philosophy in the West. According to German-American political philosopher Leo Strauss (1899–1973), philosophers have nearly always lived in times and places where their ideas would have been seen as a danger to the ruling class. As such, they had to cloak their ideas in words that seemed to express the opposite of what they intended. This is called *esoteric writing*, and at its heart lies irony. The surface obscures what's really meant; and this time it's for a good cause: to preserve a philosopher's life! And that puts *Dilbert* in good company, if you ask me.

And Then We'll Get Serious

All right. Enough chitchat around the water cooler. It's time to get back to real work and wrap up the philosophy in *Dilbert*. So, are you ready? Don't jump straight to glowering at me! Okay. Here goes: Readers of *Dilbert just don't get it*.

I mean, sure, they read *Dilbert* and get a good chuckle. They're hip to the joke, because they're both inside the situation and outside of it. Readers get the irony of experiencing the confusing, contradictory, even nonsensical white-collar workplace, no doubt about that. I mean, how couldn't they? But whereas we first looked at the structure, and then at the content, we now need to look deeper into the meaning of the irony in *Dilbert*. Since irony is the heart of *Dilbert*, it informs our understanding of what's really going on in his world—and ours.

Kierkegaard held onto the importance of irony throughout his life. We saw this first in his doctoral dissertation. But later, in *Either/Or* (1843), Kierkegaard showed that through the use of irony, we can all have a choice about how we live. We can live in the *aesthetic* world, or we can live in the *ethical* world. In the aesthetic world, it's all about *me, right now*. But by giving in to enjoying life in the moment, I actually fail to exercise any real control over my life. Sure, I'm enjoying life, and there's nothing wrong with that. Through my enjoyment, *I may even find myself feeling superior to everyone else.* But this life is an empty one because I never end up going anywhere. It's always the same old story. I never commit to building a history, a real life for myself. That's why living in an aesthetic world inevitably leads to despair.

On the other hand, in the ethical world, I can use self-reflection to get a better perspective on my situation. This allows me to take responsibility for my actions. I will then find myself making real, hard choices instead of seeking enjoyment and just living for the moment. For Kierkegaard, the bridge from the aesthetic world to the ethical world was irony. By seeking out and understanding contrasting meanings in a situation, by "getting it," irony reveals a deeper truth. With a broader perspective, more informed and better choices can be made. *Ironically, it's through making choices that we find freedom.*

Having difficulty seeing where I'm going with this? Consider: Adams has been writing *Dilbert* since 1989. For almost three decades, people have had the bizarre, confusing, nonsensical white-collar workplace revealed for what it is. *Yet nothing has changed!* This means that readers have inadvertently fallen into the trap that Hegel feared. Remember, we saw that Socrates showed that people who claim that they know something really don't. Like Socrates, Adams is neutral with respect to irony because it's up to his audience to exercise responsibility for their lives. But Hegel held that if you stopped at the irony and did not use it, you can become so involved with "getting it" that you turn inward. For Hegel, irony is negative.

Dilbert's readers do get the irony; but it's a vain, self-centered reading, *so they really don't.* The revealed message is never used to make objective changes for the better in the real world. I claim that, as Hegel warned, readers retreat into vanity as they enjoy their daily dose of *Dilbert.* Don't believe me? Read this and tell me that it doesn't sound familiar—yes, YOU, *Dilbert* fan!

This is exactly how it is in the white-collar workplace / sweatshop. My boss is a self-absorbed brain-dead noodnik who couldn't figure out two plus two without the help of a consensus at a Monday morning office meeting. My co-workers are pathetic, mindless, incompetent, back-stabbing drones. But of course, I don't behave like that.

Did Hegel use the word "vanity"? Perhaps he should have said narcissism!

To make maximum use of the irony in *Dilbert*, readers would not just have to "get" the irony, but leverage it to live better lives. They would have to be *ethical* in their reading. But by reading *Dilbert and feeling superior to everyone else,* their perspective is *narcissistic.*

After almost three decades, *Dilbert* continues to be popular. Not just because the majority of Americans find themselves working and living in that world and "getting it." It's more that nothing's changed since Adams began writing *Dilbert* in 1989. And by office workers refusing to take responsibility for all the crazy in their workday lives, America's white-collar workplace probably never will change.

When we laugh at *Dilbert*, we're all really laughing at, and fooling, ourselves. *And we should know better by now.*

Scoundrels, the lot of us. So, so irresponsible. Ironic, no?

5
The Serious Point of Scott's Humor

ENZO GUERRA AND ADAM BARKMAN

Dilbert comic strips are the artifact that we most commonly associate with Scott Adams. Dilbert, the title character, is a company man who engages in humorous, satirical exchanges with his boss, co-workers, and even his dog. Though it may seem as if these comics are intended as mere pleasure or entertainment, they also operate on another deeper level.

In his book, *How to Fail at Almost Everything and Still Win Big*, Adams says that in his Dilbert comic strips, he removes all the unnecessary noise from a situation, leaving nothing but its absurd yet essential core. Consider the following example taken from his most recent Dilbert book, *Dilbert Gets Re-Accommodated*:

> POINTY-HAIRED BOSS: Our plan is to use design psychology to make our apps more addictive. Ideally, we want to strip people of their free will and turn them into mindless upgrading zombies.
>
> DILBERT: I'd feel better if we called that "marketing."
>
> POINTY-HAIRED BOSS: I need you to be more mindless too.

Not only is this cheeky little comic strip funny, but it also shows that marketing is often concerned with manipulation-for-profit. It also reveals what is often the true nature of bosses, which is that they are controlling. Of course, this isn't meant to be the universal claim that every corporation uses addictive marketing techniques or that all bosses are controlling, but it humorously indicates that a lot of them do.

There is enough truth revealed in this comic strip to make it appropriately incisive and so avoid obvious logical fallacies. Its subtle, humorous nature goes right to the issue and elicits wide agreement, whereas if Scott Adams were simply to write an essay about the evils of manipulative marketing campaigns and controlling bosses, it might seem a bit tired or, more likely, it might be totally ignored. So humor, particularly the humor of *Dilbert* comics, can address a serious issue effectively and enjoyably, without the noise that often goes into more "seriously" addressing an issue.

Nearly all *Dilbert* comics concern the incompetencies of modern companies and their dysfunctional office workspaces. Here's another example from one of his *Dilbert* books, *Go Add Value Someplace Else*:

> WALLY: Here's my card. Let me know if I can be of further assistance.
>
> CUSTOMER: Your phone number is missing a digit and your email address doesn't have an @ symbol.
>
> WALLY: I didn't say it would be easy.

Through this comic, we see the well-attested truth that while companies are often very interested in appearing customer-friendly, many, especially when it comes to complaints, aren't. So, through an apparently simple comic, Adams uses humor to uncover an important truth about these corporations. Adams, therefore, could be seen as virtuous . . . in a way.

How Humor Can Transform Arguments

Humor can take a solemn and serious argument, and quickly communicate an insight about that argument. Here's a made-up example. The following is a type of argument sometimes expressed by philosophers expounding their thoughts on the origin of the universe:

"Nothing" as one perceives it, isn't actually nothing. Our limited minds are not capable of understanding "nothing" in its real quantum-mechanical form. Thus, what we think is nothing is not actually nothing. In fact, science reveals that "nothing" is actually something, or nothing inevitably leads to something. So you never actually have "nothing"-nothing. You always have nothing-something. Since nothing is indeed a vacuum in which particles are in chaos, it will lead to something, given enough time. Because these two are inextricably linked, you can indeed get something from nothing. Thus, the whole riddle of how the universe can come from nothing has been solved. Case closed.

Given that argument, it would be easy to get lost in all its twists and turns, especially if you read it fast. If you wanted to defeat that argument, you would have to go through the daunting task of examining each premise and seeing where you might sense logical inconsistency. However, even when you respond, you must also be ready to respond to a potential counter to your objection. And given enough time, you may even come across a whole new ad hoc argument that was developed to avoid such criticism. These debates can go on ad infinitum and even, at times, ad nauseum—to the point of barfing.

However, an alternative is there is a logical tool that could perhaps inform us about reality by piercing through these arguments with quick speed. This tool is *humor*. It's the process by which something is expressed in a comedic or amusing way, and simplifies an argument down to its crux. This allows one to see what is really being said without all the unnecessary premises, ambiguous words, and poor structures that these arguments often have.

Person A walks into their daily work office with an ice-cream cone in hand. Person B, upon observation of the ice-cream cone, asks, "Hey! Where did you get that from?"

Person A then responds, "It just popped into existence inside my hand."

Person B thinks. "At first, I thought that it is logically impossible, but then I remembered some people believe the universe did the same thing, so it can't be that absurd, right?"

The humor exposes absurdities or at least appearances of the absurd in stark relief. If nothing is literally "no-thing" devoid of any kind of properties, then it seems unlikely that it can cause anything at all. If "no-thing" is defined as chaotic chemicals and atoms in variation, then it seems as though it is a "some thing," and thus becomes not literally "no-thing."

Humor can inform us regarding reality in a quick and accessible way since it can be used as a logical tool to assess and examine arguments. Pretty cool, right? We have Scott Adams to thank for this.

An Objection to Humor as Argument

An objection to the use of humor as argument is that it can easily commit the straw man fallacy. The straw man fallacy is to represent the point of view you're criticizing in a distorted form, so that it becomes weaker and therefore easier to dismiss. Here's an example of a straw man argument:

PERSON A: I'm now a fully convinced macro-evolutionist.

PERSON B: Ha! Do you really believe that we evolved from a primordial soup?

On the surface, it seems to be using humor to refute the theory of evolution, but in fact it is a straw man argument since it ignores core Darwinian concepts like natural selection. There is more to macro-evolutionary theory than "life came from primordial soup"—it's overly simplistic and misleading in its simplicity.

So, proper humoring arguments or a proper use of humor as a logical tool needs to preserve the integrity of the claim that is being debunked. The goal still remains truthful representation, not merely a cheeky way to attack arguments that you're not fond of.

Humor as a Virtue

Not only can humor be used as a logical tool of argument, it is also a moral virtue, according to the ancient Greek philosopher Aristotle. In his *Nicomachean Ethics*, Aristotle lists humor or wittiness as one of the moral virtues, and as with every character trait, Aristotle claims there are vices—the excessive and deficient forms of these traits.

The excess of humor is the vice of "buffoonery." The person who can't be serious even when seriousness is appropriate is a buffoon; your uncle who can't stop telling jokes at a funeral is a buffoon. In the opposite direction, Aristotle condemns the deficiency of humor, the vice of "boorishness": the always-serious, only ever studying student at the library is a boor; people who can never laugh at themselves are boors. Aristotle claimed that an excellent human life included the rightly-humored character. The person who has the virtue of wittiness knows when to be serious but also when to joke.

Failing and Winning

In his book, *How to Fail at Almost Everything and Still Win Big,* Scott Adams goes through the contours of his life, highlighting everything from being a young boy with aspirations to becoming a cartoonist, to discussing the man he is today. His book pinpoints the problems he's had in life: problems with his voice, his hand, schooling, and business career. He even talks about problems with Dilbert. However in the midst of all these problems Scott shows his reader pointers and tips on how to succeed despite all the odds against you.

The humor in this book is found in the irony of his very life, and in some ways there is a very Socratic tone to it. Adams claims the people who think they are the most intelligent, most capable, and even most talented are not the ones who typically succeed—a distant echo of Socrates asking his Greek interlocutors, "You know what justice is? Fantastic! Please enlighten an ignorant man . . ." Adams proves to be a Socrates, here, by acknowledging that he is a mediocre artist, yet still one who lives comfortably as a cartoonist.

He claims that "passion," which is often the vehicle that allows a person to live the American Dream, is "bullshit." Passion is temporary. We just need to be *lucky*. He also claims that selfless, humble people can never get what they want. They must be selfish in order to get what they want. Not a kind of selfishness that is rude and mean, but a sort of Nietzschean selfishness, focusing on your life, needs, and wants above those of family, friends, and co-workers.

Scott also claims that more mediocre skills can be better than a few masterful skills. These claims seem radically different than what is often found in self-help books, where it often claims that if one wants to succeed, one must merely have a lot of ambition, and then one can accomplish anything. That may be true of a few individuals, but in reality, it's not the case for most successful people, according to Adams.

In Chapter 4, "Some of My Many Failures in Summary Form," he systematically goes through each of his failures in life. He discusses a failed attempt to create a Velcro Rosin Bag for tennis players; he discusses a meditation guide he made, which ultimately only sold three copies; and he discusses many other failures like computer games, websites, and perhaps most comedic, the Dilberito, which was a healthy food product that contained a lot of your daily vitamins, and which was ultimately sold to another corporation.

Adams claims that it isn't about ideas, which can be good, but about being *lucky*. In fact, in Chapter 25, he claims that the whole Dilbert enterprise was the result of luck. He maintains that if events had not lined up with others in the way he describes, this book regarding Adams probably wouldn't have been written because he probably would not have been as well-known as he is today.

The absurd but true core lies in the fact that our capitalist society has given its members a false impression of how to succeed, and Adams humorously shows that he himself should be a "failure" of some sort. If you want to succeed, try to increase your odds of being lucky. OF COURSE, we should not take this to be his real point; rather, his point is that The American Dream is an over-sell.

Win Bigly

In his book *Win Bigly: Persuasion in a World Where Facts Don't Matter*, Scott Adams talks about the ancient art of persuasion, more specifically, persuasion in the political realm. He establishes that there are three levels of persuaders.

First, there are the amateur persuaders like himself, who probably know a fair bit more than the average Joe. Second, you have the cognitive scientists, who know more about persuasion by virtue of knowing the mind and how it works. And lastly, there are the master persuaders, who are very rare and operate in a whole different dimension.

Though Scott makes it clear that he doesn't agree with any one political side, he admires Donald Trump's persuasion skills, which are indeed master grade. In fact, Adams predicted that Trump would win primarily because of his persuasion skills. Throughout the book, Adams brings you through the contours of his prediction of Trump's victory and ultimately outlines how to become a better persuader. Aristotle would be proud of him.

The humor in *Win Bigly* is the paradoxical nature of humans, especially in the realm of politics. Scott claims that human beings are deluded when they think most of their choices and opinions are the result of rational reflection. In fact, Adams argues that we each have this subjective filter in which we interpret reality. He even cites Hume and Kant in support of this idea.

Scott claims that humans are inevitably the result of two psychological theories. Firstly, we all suffer from cognitive dissonance, which is the attempt to rationalize why one's actions are different from one's beliefs and values. And secondly, we're all victims of confirmation bias, which is the tendency to view all evidence as supporting our own views. Thus, it is possible, according to Adams, for people to be looking at the exact same data, and draw different conclusions.

In a world where people simply experience life through their own subjective lens, facts become overrated. Because facts are interpreted differently, you can't convince someone else of a different position by facts alone. In fact, proposing objections can strengthen the other person's view and even make it more difficult to sway them.

So what's the method by which politicians get what they want and sway people into making their campaign seem ideal? Persuasion! It's not about what you say. It's about how you say it. If you can get your ideas across in a persuasive way, then you can pretty much win a presidential election. Trump, according to Adams, won because of his persuasion skills.

Now you might stop for a moment and ask yourself whether or not this framework reduces the political system to a battle of sophistry instead of truth. Sadly, but humorously, according to Adams, this is so. It's the reason why he humorously provides thirty-one tips throughout the book on how to become a better persuader. Trump was shown to be a master persuader because of the following: he was a proponent of intentional mistakes (so as to attract attention); he displayed a strong sense of confidence; he was well-dressed (formal dress appears to give a sense of credibility and authority); he used visual imagery (which is more powerful and effective than just verbal imagery); he used repetition, which would ultimately stick with his supporters and his critics; and so on. Though Scott makes it clear that he doesn't support the political ideas of either Trump or Clinton, he does admire Trump's persuasion skills.

The rub, of course, is that the humor here—the over-selling of the importance of persuasion—is meant to be instructive rather than literal. It's not that persuasion is so great—Hitler was a great persuader, too—but rather that cold, rational arguments are often ineffective in making signigicant change and that, we think, is Adams's real point.

So, by attending to the core, central truth on a given issue and then applying this to a humorous situation—with a great dose of irony—Scott Adams demonstrates that he not only has the Aristotelian virtue of wit but also the Socratic demeanor to go along with it.

6
The PowerPoint Conspiracy Theory

CHRISTOPHER KETCHAM

William of Ockham, a Franciscan monk from the twelfth century, said that given two or more hypotheses that explain something, the one with the fewest assumptions is likely the better hypothesis. This is minimalist thinking. Why take one more step than you must?

See, this is the point of PowerPoint. Make the footprint small and the typeset HUGE so you can't stuff too much onto the page. William of Ockham would have loved PowerPoint.

On the other hand, the PowerPoint type size gets smaller and smaller the more you try to stuff on the tiny page. At some point it just gives up and begs you to make a new slide. In the twentieth century Rube Goldberg produced contraptions that used many more steps than necessary to pour a cup of coffee, or toast a piece of bread. This is maximalist thinking. Are you a PowerPoint minimalist or a maximalist?

Dostoevsky's *Crime and Punishment* is four hundred-plus pages, many thousands of words. A Scott Adams cartoon may consist of three to six panels and be less than fifty words. Cartoonists must think minimally with just the right combination of art and words to make their statement. We can debate the value of the work of Dostoevsky against Adams but in the end, Adams achieves his message in a minimalist way and Dostoyevsky takes the long route. How about Dickens, "It was the best of times; it was the worst of times," or

Melville, "Call me Ishmael," both perfect PowerPoint phrases? How did Dickens and Melville know how to do this? Folks, it's in our genes.

About Minimalism

Before we get to the conspiracy that is PowerPoint, we must take a historical deep dive to tease out its primitive origins. Minimalism does not begin with Ockham. We see minimalism in the very real but simple prehistoric cave paintings. Sometimes it's just an animal and a palm print. In other words, a painting signed by the author. In the twentieth century, musical composers like John Adams, John Cage, and Philip Glass composed music from simple chord progressions that are highly repetitive. Cage's 4' 33" has no notes; it's four minutes and thirty-three seconds of ambient noise—but not all agree on its minimalism because noise is quite complex. In 1915, Kazimir Malevich, paints a black square . . . that's right, a black square.

For many people, minimalist art and music is so much nonsense. Perhaps it is . . . However, have we not been conditioned to minimalist thinking in other ways? The billboard. The street sign—STOP. The cartoon. The words, "no" . . . and "yes," and the PowerPoint presentation, the canvas "of the people, by the people, and for the people"—you see now, don't you, even Lincoln was a minimalist. We can go too far. That is where this conspiracy thing comes in. Oh, and we will get to Scott Adams presently, just be patient.

Points about PowerPoint

PowerPoint was purportedly designed for business, for the time challenged and hopelessly perplexed executive who undoubtedly cannot understand any report unless it is distilled down into pithy one-line bullet points in large print. Think child psychology.

The large print means that we're to assume that once again we are in a kindergarten class, writing letters with three-line ruled paper so that we can carefully keep the circle of the small letter 'd' within the first two lines (the thick bottom one and the dotted one above) and extend the tail of the 'd' to the thick top line but no higher. MY NAME IS JILL. See how easy it is? It tells you everything you need to know about the child. Her name is Jill. What do we need to know about the child beyond that? What does your corporate executive need to know? Probably not much more than that.

We all know that Dilbert has a most ineffective boss. You know him, he who is always proposing stupid stuff or damning good stuff. And he speaks Gobbledygook Business (GB), the language that has no dictionary. So, when the Pointy-Haired Boss said in September 2014, "Executives only respond to familiar colors and shapes," you know he's singing the praise of PowerPoint itself. As I said, it's in our genes, even in the too-many-chromosomes Pointy-Haired Boss.

Most business problems do not involve nuclear physics, but when it comes to things like logistics, IT, actuarial analysis, economics, and finance, the execs are probably not going to be well-versed in each of these various business sciences. Simplicity is advised. This is why Microsoft created Power-Point as an unpretentious tool to be used by the masses. However, once the corporate geek starts playing with the program we're apt to experience anything from a child's stick-figure representation of his family, to something elegantly fashioned to convince a busy executive to decide more quickly, and hopefully make a better decision.

Yet, there's no hope even this will work with the Pointy Haired Boss. He likely will make the worst possible decision and send the office down a rabbit hole of useless work, toil, trouble, and with an impossible deadline. You've been down this rabbit hole, haven't you?

Can we assume that Microsoft had Ockham in mind? As we will see, not in the way that Ockham saw his minimalist maxim. For example, in July 2011 when the Pointy-Haired Boss tries to build his own PowerPoint deck, Dilbert asks questions about what he wants. The Boss's response? Too many questions. Well, what about Dilbert? See, he's confined to a cubicle—just about the same size as the PowerPoint footprint in one of those open offices where the walls are short and people peer over them. This is where the term talking head comes from. What a world, what a small and inconsequential world.

So, is Adams also a victim of PowerPointlessness? The horror, the horror (Yeah, Joseph Conrad's *The Heart of Darkness* . . . or the movie *Apocalypse Now*). You see now how pervasive this minimalist thing is?

PowerPoint Etiquette

PowerPoint etiquette suggests that you keep the bullet points per slide to three and the sentence to one line, if it needs to be a sentence. "My name is Jill" is a great example of an informative PowerPoint bullet point. However, business-speak, jargon, acronyms, and the gobbledygook you get from a presentation on new software, the cloud, cybersecurity, and even from the new workspace office designer, are for the most part indecipherable even if written in cozy one-liners.

Then there is the aggressive PowerPoint junkie who pours her heart into the program, producing lurid graphics of competing colors, flashing things, and way too many lines of code—bullet points per slide. Slide transitions—always annoying. These are the crammers. Their slides are like looking at a wall of graffiti: much ado about nothing; or if it is something, not something I will ever get. In an August 2008 Adams cartoon, Wally crams all his material onto one slide which is as black as Malevich's black square. So, what's it with Wally? He's a schemer. He is an antiestablishment hero of sorts, though he is quite ineffectual. His life's goal is to figure out how to game the system to his advantage, of course. However, this usually backfires or blows up in his face.

I am worried now. I just counted. Adams's website has fifty-six cartoon strips where PowerPoint is a key word. You think he's obsessed? Has he been taken in by PowerPoint—and not in a good way? It is possible.

The Iranian Connection

Now take Dogbert, the anti-hero pup who dogs Dilbert. Who else could come up with a conspiracy theory but Dogbert? That's his stock in trade. In one *Dilbert* strip in June of 2007, Dogbert suggests to Dilbert that Dilbert's company funds terrorists. Dilbert makes a flimsy excuse that they aren't bad terrorists to which Dogbert asks how Dilbert became brainwashed so quickly . . . The Iranians gave the terrorists PowerPoint, says Dilbert.

You think that the Pointy-Haired-Boss will love this? Do you think he will understand the implications? No, he'll jump on it and push everyone but himself into taking Persian lessons. Then when Wally produces a PowerPoint presentation full of Persian looking gibberish, the Pointy Haired Boss will nod authoritatively . . . You get the picture.

This suggests that there can be a dark side to PowerPoint and minimalism in general. Ockham, recall, said that given two good and complete explanations, we should choose the one with the fewest assumptions. The issues we must discuss are *good* and *complete*. Turning back to Jill. You just met her, and she says, "My mommy is a nurse" rather than give her own name. That could be, but we know nothing about Jill other than that she appears to be a little girl. We have too few assumptions or answers in this case to know who this little girl is other than that her mommy is a nurse. We have less than what's necessary to make even a minimalist assumption. With this revelation, however, we have only scratched the surface. Much more lies hidden . . . which I will soon reveal.

Now to the Iranians. Washington is like an enormous washing machine on perpetual spin cycle. In recent months we have been subjected to fake news, meddling, click-bait "journalism," alternative facts, sound-bite reporting, conspiracy theories, and other jargon (did I say there was no collusion?) that leaves us with the notion that we do not have enough information to make a good decision on just about anything that flies out of the Washington spin machine. This is the peril of minimalism: too little information. We can dismiss the news, or do research, or listen to other takes on what happened, but in the end, we remain unnerved that, like a pretzel without salt, we are missing something important.

Microsoft isn't the only culprit in this dive towards minimalism. Most text apps trim messages into 160 characters; Twitter stops out now at 280. Both are simple versions of PowerPoint with a twist, restrictions against cramming the slide with too much stuff. Is 280 characters enough to satisfy Ockham? Maybe, if "My name is Jill" is all you need to know. However, we have political leaders, political wannabees, pundits, and critics who try to explain public policy, complicated news, and other things using the Tweet. Certainly, Ockham was speaking about brevity, but not at the expense of the assumptions required to formulate a good answer. So where did this dive to minimalism come from?

It Came From DARPA! (Coming Soon to a Theater Near You)

It came from DARPA (Defense Advanced Research Projects Agency), the black operations arm of the defense department that cooks up James Bond–like contraptions and other devices, programs, and tools of defense and offense used in both cold and hot wars. They've hitched mines to porpoises, used pigeons to guide bombs, designed hypersonic aircraft, done a lot of stuff with programming, including worms, viruses, and other invasive or disruptive hacks. They are presumed to be behind the Stuxnet worm that sent Iranian centrifuges to spin into self-destruction. How apropos that Washington's spin cycle could destroy something.

I know that Scott Adams knows that DARPA was behind PowerPoint. We can see it in the code words in *Dilbert*, like: engineering and puppet (April 2011), infinite turtles as in the creation myth that the earth is a turtle and there are turtles all the way down (February 2011), portal to another dimension (September 2011), garbage and flies—think bugs, worms, hacking (September 2011). That's just in 2011. And you didn't see the conspiracy when you read these, did you? Tisk, tisk.

The whole PowerPoint conspiracy theory begins like a good DARPA mystery thriller. Why is PowerPoint not two words? Why is it pushed together, and why does it have two capitals? Early researchers brushed this off as a holdover from Microsoft DOS days, when you got that annoying %20 every time you used a space. Remember DOS . . . as in . . . Format c: y (look it up!). Even *that* cannot erase this annoying PowerPoint conspiracy.

Others claim that since other programs of Microsoft Office are one word, PowerPoint needs to be one word. What they all miss is the coded message in the word itself—Power. That's right, with a capital P. It was this simple explanation (Thank you, Ockham) that sent me down the path to where I could finally understand the implications of the program and what it means to human civilization. It was a code word for something much dastardlier, as you are about to find out.

You see, there is even a deeper secret than 'Power', one that is just becoming known. You can hear the rumors and rumbles of this throughout the Internet and beyond, but it is in the form of broken code, misleading tweets, click-bait advertising, and on a billboard outside of Atlanta that references a cold beverage that will not be named. All these seemingly inconsequential bits of information do fit together quite nicely to explain the origin of PowerPoint and how DARPA was involved. Yes, the simplest explanation is the best, and quite frankly, there is no simpler explanation than I am about to give you. However, while the explanation is simple, the bumpy ride that is the history of PowerPoint will bruise your bones and put a chill down the skin on your back—goosebumps will rise for a very important reason.

From the Gulag to the Suburbs

It came by way of Siberia. We now have incontrovertible proof that DARPA engineered PowerPoint in collaboration with Microsoft in 1990 to take down the Soviet Union.

Vladimir Putin, then a KGB spook, discovered PowerPoint and its mind-numbing power but did nothing about it. He wanted power for himself, you see. Well we all know what happened. After PowerPoint slowed the economy and brought down the Soviet Union, Putin let PowerPoint run rampant through the Russian economy, to simplify it, by eliminating the Soviet five-year plan nonsense so that money could be made. But this also produced Boris Yeltsin, the first democratic President of post-soviet Russia. He was, you might say, a buffoon. Yeltsin was Putin's next great leap to assert the power he possessed by hacking PowerPoint and its code.

Before he even came to power, Putin had his fellow cyber-spooks rewrite the PowerPoint code so that the oligarchs he created would funnel money into his bank account. Well, becoming the wealthiest person on the planet wasn't enough. Riding shirtless through the steppes like a rugged Cossack, wasn't enough. Above all, Putin is about Power, naked, raw, sociopathic Power. He tried for years, even before he came to Power, to influence American politics through his cyber-infected code that produced stupid. How close did he come? He came close with Bill Clinton who asked what "is" is. He got closer still with Bush II and his obsession with imaginary weapons of mass destruction. He got the Birthers to spread the word about Obama . . . Then came Donald Trump.

The Trump Factor

Trump, with his short attention span, became obsessed with how simple PowerPoint made the world seem. After being conditioned by PowerPoint, Trump naturally took to Twitter and has saved the US Government Printing Office millions of dollars because he can no longer read anything more than a tweet. We now know he gained this ability from becoming conditioned to see only the magical bullet point that produces a simple take on the complexities of the world. How did he get elected? He told the American people, who have also been conditioned by PowerPoint, what they wanted to hear, using bullet point simplicities like: disaster, great, so sad, fake news, crooked, and total hoax. Thank you, Mr. Putin.

You see, Russian meddling wasn't about the elections per se. Putin didn't rig voting machines. He rigged Trump. PowerPoint is the only connection between Trump and Russia. Breitbart and Fox News and all the others in Trump's circle are right to condemn any idea of collusion. Trump did it to himself, and well, of course, with the tangential assistance of Putin and his shadowy operatives.

Dilbert and Truth

You want proof. You need to look no further than the pages of *Dilbert*: <http://dilbert.com/search_results?terms=powerpoint>. This link is dangerous because it will take you to the archives of PowerPoint cartoons that in truly minimalist terms will explain in more detail than I have room for in this chapter how DARPA and Microsoft conspired to create a mechanism to reintroduce stupid into the world.

PowerPoint, a regressive and retro-seeking program, has done more to disable the intellectual capacity of humans than any lobotomy conducted in the 1930s in the cause of ending schizophrenia. Perversely, PowerPoint de-evolution requires no genetic engineering, just a return to abject minimalism when a grunt meant something to the caveman. The spawn of PowerPoint, texts, and tweets, and their rigid adherence to character limits have only served to enforce the stupid that Gates, Microsoft, and DARPA used to make the Russians forget their ambitions, let go of their hold on Eastern Europe, and to disremember all they had learned on how to be good Communists. No engineered bird flu virus or Stuxnet worm could have done more damage than PowerPoint.

Now, I won't regale you with too much evidence. You must go to the *Dilbert* website and do this yourself. However, I will give you some of the Ockham-rich assumptions that you will find in Adams's work. We already have seen the coded Iran message and the black square message (think black ops). Here are more.

Take Asok. Remember him? He's Indian, like, from India, but that doesn't matter to the story. He's quite smart and can solve problems just as simply as William of Ockham. However, he gets abused by his office mates because he is a nerd and can't hide anything. He is a Brainiac with a flexible nose. How often does Asok's nose grow when he is around Power-Point, and doesn't that mean that we should all be embarrassed by lies? Yet, is it a lie if we have too little information? What about coma or hypnotic trances after viewing a PowerPoint presentation? Right there in Adams's work.

In August 2000, after Dilbert shows slide 397, where the audience have suddenly become violently ill, Wally says, "PowerPoint poisoning." In February 2012 Dilbert explains to the Pointy-Haired Boss, "For my intelligent viewers, I have data and for morons I have manipulative anecdotes." In December 2005, in his cubicle, Dilbert says, "I am entering the PowerPoint Zone." Eat your heart out, Rod Sterling.

Finally, in June 2010, after his audience have all fallen into a PowerPoint coma, Dilbert says, "The only thing I can do now is put them into funny poses and leave." How often have you left a PowerPoint presentation and felt like someone had done something really nasty to you and that everyone was laughing behind your back? You see, right there in the pages of *Dilbert*.

Certainly, DARPA's had something to do with this. Phil appears in these strips and we know that when Phil appears, something devilish is about to occur . . . Known as "the prince of insufficient light," who else but Phil would pull a prank like getting everyone to use PowerPoint? Can't you see him dissolve crystal meth in Wally's coffee to make him produce a massively overwritten PowerPoint slide, or fill his jelly donut with some psychedelic substance so he can produce that marvelous Persian-like gibberish?

Shall I go on? I believe I must. For we must understand that throughout his body of work on the PowerPoint conspiracy, Adams consistently shows how the slide deck (yeah, slang for PowerPoint) is being used to create stupid, wasted effort, inefficiency, alternative facts, and just-plain nonsense.

Projects become mush and department results become incomprehensible, if not complete fabrications.

Now, I have it on good authority that DARPA had originally desired PowerPoint to be only a Russian program. Unfortunately, it's gone viral and proliferates like the flu. Microsoft continues to mutate it to make it increasingly more "useful" (translated stupid-producing) to unsuspecting people like you and me . . . Just like the flu that captures your attention every winter, PowerPoint remains deeply embedded in your mind as a tool for making stupid—though until now, you didn't see it that way, did you? In fact, it mutates so often, that like the flu virus, you don't have time to make antibodies against becoming dumber. Twitter and texting only exacerbate stupid.

You've seen it, the Zombie syndrome infecting most of our youth today. Bent over, staring at small screens, they shuffle from classroom to classroom to see, you guessed it, another PowerPoint presentation. Their minds have been dulled to short attention spans and clips of characters that make little sense. They even have created their own code, acronyms, and nonsense words to explain stupid in texts and Tweets. All because a DARPA program got out of hand.

Is there a *Dilbert* app for your phone, child zombie phones? Not yet, but you think the cartoon would fit on a phone screen? Gasp, the conspiracy is everywhere. Is nothing sacred? After Trump? Not much.

Full Stop NOW!

You've got facts in hand, more research to do, and a sinking feeling that all has not been right with the world for some time now. It's time to put all of this into its proper place, and that is with philosophical theory. Something that we can stuff into a minimalist box. To counteract the underlying untruths that set PowerPoint on its journey into our psyche, we must have truths. How about moral realism as our theory? Sure, if it isn't a fact, an objective, incontrovertible fact, moral realists cannot say it is moral or not moral. The problem is that, in the murky world of conspiracies, it is most difficult to distinguish the truth from sort of the truth, wannabe truths, and outright lies.

Within moral realism is the idea of minimalism—that is, we cannot assert anything beyond what has been initially said about the act's morality or not. John lied about his age. Okay, fine enough. Moral or not moral? John has no birth certificate. He guesses his age. Is that a lie? Argh.

See, it is not just about the 'truth' but it is also about context. So, we can't get to moral realism yet from this pesky PowerPoint conspiracy that seems to mangle and mingle the truth with lies, slights, and even fake news. What about other theories? Immanuel Kant says we cannot lie even if it is to save someone else from harm. Do we really want to go there? How about the notion from utilitarianism that the best moral decision is one where the greatest happiness for the greatest number of people is achieved? So, to increase productivity the Pointy-Haired Boss has everyone smoke crack. Everyone is really happy . . . Naw, too expensive.

You got it, we don't have enough information to use any existing moral theory or develop our own yet . . . and that's just what the conspiracy-minded minimalists want us to think about PowerPoint. It's a Lazarus program, the resurrection of stupid. This is why Adams continually bombards us with his brief and colorful missives in *Dilbert* about the stupid that is the nature of PowerPoint. Folks, PowerPoint is the tool that lets loose moral realism in the form of twisted minimalism, incomplete minimalism, and misleading minimalism. It unleashed the urban legend and floods our airways with conspiracy theories for which we have incomplete information with which to judge their moral claims.

Back to Scott Adams once again. In a January 2010 strip, Dilbert explains that through the new technology being proposed the company can be managed by two monkeys, one to manage and one to look at PowerPoint slides. If we do not want to return to our simian roots, we need to begin to boycott PowerPoint. I mean, throw it to the floor. Well, that wasn't too bright was it? The laptop is now destroyed. Delete it then, go to uninstall and uninstall it. Reject as spam any PowerPoint you are sent by e-mail. Tell your friends on Facebook, Twitter, Tumblr, and Snapchat to do the same. Reject *Homo stupidus* to become *Homo sapiens* once again. If we all do this, we can eradicate minimalism and its minions, PowerPoint, Twitter, and Text just as we have done with smallpox. It's time to send DARPA and their warped sense of moral realism packing. Spin them back to their lair in Foggy Bottom.

Be like Dilbert in the February 2010 strip when he realizes during his work week he produced nothing but useless PowerPoint slides. He screams in agony at the thought, "My brain is eating my body . . ."

I've said enough. Do your own research. Me? I'm off to Facebook to post a picture of a plate of food I'm going to eat tonight.

III

---

*It Tastes Better if We
All Do It Together*

7
Scott Adams's Joy of Logic

RICHARD BILSKER

Among the morbid delights of the *Dilbert* comic strip are the delicious instances of bad thinking displayed by the Pointy-Haired Boss. In his book, *The Joy of Work: Dilbert's Guide to Finding Happiness at the Expense of Your Co-Workers*, Scott Adams includes a chapter called "Managing Your Co-Workers." This has long been a favorite of mine and its ideas have found their way into logic classes I have taught over many years.

After discussing such heady topics as cubicle flatulence and office moves, the chapter has a section on "Dealing with Irrational Co-Workers." This section includes instances of logical fallacies and cognitive biases interspersed with *Dilbert* strips. Understanding these examples can certainly help you to become a better critical thinker.

Cognitive Biases and Logical Fallacies

Paul Herrick has described cognitive biases as psychological obstacles to critical thinking. They are patterns of pre-logical thinking that make it harder for us to use reason to draw conclusions. Though there are some controversies regarding the number of biases and their extent, there is an evolving set of biases recognized (and tested for) by psychologists and behavioral economists. Some, like being self-centered (egocentric) or being susceptible to prejudice, have been long recognized.

Fallacies are errors in reasoning. Formal fallacies are problems with logical structure in systems of deduction. Informal fallacies are patterns of reasoning that are so common that many of the oldest have been discussed since the medieval period and are commonly still referred to by their Latin names.

Irrational Co-Workers (and Others)

In "Dealing with Irrational Co-Workers," Scott Adams gives us a humorous lesson in critical thinking. In most cases, he has changed the names . . . but probably not to protect the innocent. As he notes, "Nothing can reduce your happiness faster than an argument with an irrational co-worker." His solution: since "irrational people are easily persuaded by anything that has been published," use his book as the publication that persuades them they are wrong! Just photocopy this section of the book ("You Are Wrong Because . . .") and circle the number of the appropriate example. He provides thirty-two examples. Here are some I have found most instructive.

Analogy Arguments

Analogy arguments are an important part of science and law. When drugs are tested on animals, the only reason to draw conclusions about humans is based on the similarities between the relevant biological systems of these species. The same is true in law when a judge has to make a ruling on allowing evidence, for example. Is the instance in front of me, she must consider, more like the precedent in *U.S. v Jones* or more like the precedent in *U.S. v Smith*? However, as the saying goes, you shouldn't compare apples and oranges.

A common fallacy is "faulty analogy." This is a catch-all description for analogies that do not consider relevant features or circumstances. Adams's example is called "Amazingly Bad Analogy" and goes like this: "You can train a dog to fetch a stick. Therefore, you can train a potato to dance." The problem here is that not enough (or any, really) relevant similarities between dogs and potatoes have been illustrated. Adams has another faulty analogy example called "Irrelevant Comparisons": "A hundred dollars is a good price for a toaster, compared to buying a Ferrari." Toasters to Ferraris is another kind of apples to oranges (or dogs to potatoes) example.

The English philosopher Sir Francis Bacon (1561–1626) is often credited with laying out some of the basics of scientific method. He can also be credited with this bad analogy in his essay, "Of the True Greatness of Kingdoms and Estates":

> No body can be healthful without exercise, neither natural body nor politic; and certainly to a kingdom or estate, a just and honorable war is the true exercise. A civil war, indeed, is like the heat of a fever; but a foreign war is like the heat of exercise, and serveth to keep the body in health; for in a slothful peace, both courages will effeminate and manners corrupt.

Much like Toasters/Ferraris, Apples/Oranges, and Dogs/Potatoes, Human Body/Body Politic do not compare. It's also not clear what justifies the analogy within an analogy here. How is civil war like a fever and a foreign war like exercise? He does not elaborate.

Causal Arguments

Causal arguments are constructed to give us good reason to accept some conclusion of the form "C caused E." You might want to know why a group of people in a particular region all developed similar symptoms. What, if anything did they have in common? What did they do differently from family members who didn't have those symptoms? If you pay attention to the news, you may often note that *E. coli* or some other bacteria was found in some food source the victims were all exposed to at some point. The headline might be something like "*E. coli* in Burger Meat Found to be the Cause of Local Deaths and Hospitalizations." Causal arguments are common in science.

One common problem is "confusing correlation with cause." A positive correlation is when you note that the presence of something seems to go with some other thing being present, too. A negative correlation is when the presence of something seems to go with the absence of some other thing (or when A goes up, B goes down). In economics, it is often said that unemployment rates and inflation rates are negatively correlated.

Adams's example is called "Faulty Cause and Effect": "On the basis of my observations, wearing huge pants make you fat." When two things are correlated, there are four possibilities. Either A caused B, B caused A, A and B are both caused by some third thing C, or lastly, it is coincidence. Ideally, to determine cause, you need to rule out the other three possibilities. That seems to be what happened in the Adams example. While it's true that wearing large pants is correlated with being overweight, it is more likely from a causal standpoint that being overweight is responsible for the size of the pants, rather than the other way around. Let's look at a recent example that has had more widespread impact than Adams's huge pants.

Economists Carmen Reinhart and Kenneth Rogoff claimed in a 2010 paper, that carrying too much debt caused a nation's economic growth to slow. According to their data, which were not published in the article itself, when the debt-to-GDP ratio of a nation crosses the threshold of ninety percent, growth slows. Their conclusion was used as an impetus for what are called austerity measures by Paul Ryan in the United States (his budget and "Path to Prosperity") and by George Osborne who was Chancellor of the Exchequer in the United Kingdom from 2010 to 2016.

Austerity typically means you cut government spending to reduce the debt. Usually social services are among the first cuts. So, austerity can have wide-ranging consequences. In 2013, Thomas Herndon, Michael Ash, and Robert Pollin, three economists at the University of Massachusetts-

Amherst published a working paper (using data provided to them by Reinhart and Rogoff) that points out a number of flaws in the Reinhart and Rogoff paper. One problem is that the data do not show cause, but only correlation. Paul Krugman, the 2008 Nobel Prize–winner for Economics, goes further and argues that it seems in several cases debt only goes up *after* the growth slows.

Another fallacy is "complex cause." This occurs when you oversimplify a situation down to one cause out of many, typically a minor one or one favored by the speaker. This is common in arguments by politicians, when they want to focus on one thing that their party is against. Adams's version is "Inability to Understand that Some Things Have Multiple Causes": "The Beatles were popular for one reason only: They were good singers." Much like the causes of World War I, there were many factors responsible for the popularity of The Beatles.

"Objectionable (or false) cause" is a catch-all fallacy for drawing a causal conclusion from too little causal evidence. Adams gives us "Reaching Bizarre Conclusions without Any Information": "The car won't start. I'm certain the spark plugs have been stolen by rogue clowns." Presumably, your co-worker made this proclamation before checking whether the spark plugs are still there. Without any really good evidence, this probably is not the first move you should make.

In 1965 Gilbert Harman named a form of inductive argument called Inference to the Best Explanation. The hallmark of this kind of argument is that you start with what you want to explain (or determine the cause of) and then consider what might possibly explain it. Then using some criteria such as simplicity, explanatory power, and consistency, narrow it down to the one that seems best based on the currently available data. Many, if not most, of the episodes of the television show *House* were a series of Inferences to the Best Explanation. Dr. House and his team would be presented with a medical enigma. They would list all the features of the mystery and toss around ideas of what condition would explain the phenomena. Once they had chosen the best one, they would treat the patient based on the diagnosis. If the treatment didn't work, they could eliminate one possible cause and also add new information to the data for a new round of diagnosis.

The criterion of simplicity (sometimes called "parsimony" or "elegance") is the idea that if you can explain something with a simpler hypothesis it is better to do so than to rely on a more complicated one. This was part of Copernicus's motivation for the heliocentric theory, for example (though his finished product was more complicated).

A famous name for this principle is Occam's Razor and was named for medieval English philosopher William of Ockham (around 1287–1347). He said something like "Don't multiply entities without necessity." The razor is to "shave" off the unnecessary. This idea, too, gets the Adams treatment as "Overapplication of Occam's Razor": "The simplest explanation for the moon landings is that they were hoaxes."

The problem here is that is not clear *how* this would be simpler. Given the number of people involved in the work (NASA, the media, ordinary people who witnessed the launches, and so forth), it looks as if a hoax would be much less *simple*. A good friend of mine who is a project manager at NASA *still* gets emails about hoaxes and conspiracies. History shows it is very hard to keep people quiet long enough to have a successful conspiracy.

Another example that is similar is "Ignoring All Anecdotal Evidence": "I always get hives immediately after eating strawberries. But without a scientifically controlled experiment, it's not reliable data. So, I continue to eat strawberries every day, since I can't tell if they cause hives." This is another piece of poor causal reasoning that violates Occam's Razor and probably IBE standards, too.

Authority

One handy shortcut based on the availability of accumulated sciences, is that you do not need to do all the science yourself. If there is widespread (near-unanimous) agreement about something, you are able to argue for a conclusion based on expert authority, provided that your chosen expert is a respected authority in their field, representative of that widespread agreement, and is speaking within their area of expertise. Examples might include Albert Einstein on relativity theory or Stephen Hawking on cosmology.

The "Fallacy of Misplaced Authority" occurs when your chosen representative does not meet the standards mentioned above. In 1986, an actor from the soap opera *All My Children* was in an ad for Vicks 44, a cough suppressant. In the ad, Peter Bergman utters the line, "I'm not a doctor, but I play one on TV." The implication is that playing a doctor is close enough.

Scott Adams gives us "Following the Advice of Known Idiots": "Uncle Billy says pork makes you smarter. That's good enough for me!" Nothing stated here makes Uncle Billy an expert in either nutrition or cognition. At the same time, Adams does not provide any reasons to call Uncle Billy a "known idiot."

Begging the Question

The fallacy of "begging the question" occurs when an argument asserts the conclusion as one of its premises. Usually, it is not so bold as to use the same exact words. A simple example would be concluding someone is famous based on the premise that they are well-known. The problem arises because "well-known" and "famous" are synonymous. Circular arguments (or vicious circles) are often described as a subset of question-begging. The circle may be small or large, but the logical form might be something like A because B. How do you know B? Because C. How do you know C? Because A.

A common example would be "Scientology is the correct way to view the universe. It clearly says so in *Dianetics*." Adams does not have a funny name for his version, but his example is one we have probably all heard from a co-worker at some point in our working life. "Circular Reasoning": "I'm correct because I'm smarter than you. And I must be smarter than you because I'm correct." Question-begging and vicious circles are not helpful because you are not given any reason to accept the conclusion that is not the conclusion itself (or outside the circle).

Cognitive Biases

The Joy of Work also has some examples that might be better described as cognitive biases. My favorite is one Scott Adams calls "I Am the World": "I don't listen to country music. Therefore, country music is not popular." This has similarities to the biases of "egocentrism" (I count more than others), "first-person bias" (evaluating the good of others based on the good for us), and "false consensus" (the idea that there is widespread agreement about something when there isn't). There are also similarities to what is often called "the psychologist's fallacy" (the "similar to me" stereotype).

Stereotyping is another bias. Adams has a version of this called "The Few Are the Same as the Whole": "Some Elbonians are animal rights activists. Some Elbonians wear fur coats. Therefore, Elbonians are hypocrites." This example also has the problem of violating one of the rules for categorical arguments. Namely that you cannot have an "all" conclusion if both your premises have "some."

Confirmation Bias

One of the running themes in Scott Adams's most recent book, *Win Bigly: Persuasion in a World Where Facts Don't Matter*, is confirmation bias. Paul Herrick describes confirmation bias as "the unconscious tendency to look harder for confirming evidence than for disconfirming evidence when investigating a matter." Typically, this occurs when we have a vested interest in what we are trying to confirm. There are instances of confirmation bias in the 2010 Reinhart and Rogoff paper mentioned above. This was not discovered until 2013 when Herndon, Ash, and Pollin got access to the data. It seems that Reinhart and Rogoff cherry-picked their data excluding some that did not support their claims. Further, there were math errors that suggested that growth does slow with higher carried debt, but instead of the negative growth (–0.1 percent) that they claimed, growth only slowed to 2.2 percent, which is not significantly slower growth than the 2.8 percent they claimed for the 60–90 percent debt ratio.

By the time these errors were found, people were already using their data for policy decisions. In fact, those who supported austerity did not change their tune once the new data was published. This, too, is confirmation bias. For Adams, confirmation bias is a big part of explaining Donald Trump's win in the 2016 election and why his supporters do not change their minds about him. Facts don't matter. As he puts it, "People don't change opinions about emotional topics just because some information proved their opinion to be nonsense. Humans aren't wired that way."

When discussing cognitive biases in my classes, I point out that they are *unconscious*, pre-logical patterns. The best we can do is become aware of them and try not to let them into our *conscious* logical thinking. On this view, cognitive biases are like programs running in the background of your computer. Adams sees it more radically. To him, the bias "isn't an occasional bug in our human operating system. It *is* the operating system." If he is right, then much of our attempt at being better critical thinkers is a waste of time. So would be our attempts to reason with our co-workers, or anyone else, about the world.

Hardwired for Nonsense?

When *The Joy of Work* was published, I was already a fan of *Dilbert*. I found the examples in the text useful for teaching logical fallacies, because they are more extreme examples than the ones found in logic textbooks which tend to be rather dry. Twenty years on, I still find the chapter to be highly entertaining.

I have a different reaction to *Win Bigly*. Much of the book is concerned with how Scott Adams was able to predict what seemed at the time to be the long shot of a Trump victory.

Other parts of the book explain the success of Trump's speaking style, which to the academic ear often sounds like nonsense. Although I take many of the pronouncements in *Win Bigly* with a grain of salt, I worry about the implications. What if we really are hardwired to accept nonsense as long as it's presented in a certain way? What if the fact that I think I'm not susceptible to these persuasion techniques is just me patting myself on the back while I fall into different (but similar traps)? There are no easy answers here.

My takeaway is that I think Adams overstates how incapable we are of overcoming biases. If Adams really is as good a "commercial grade persuader" as he tells us throughout the book, would he really need to restate it so often? I recommend that you read *Win Bigly* and draw your own conclusions. Aside from that, I recommend that you enjoy *Dilbert* strips and *The Joy of Work*—and try to avoid the common critical thinking traps I've mentioned here.

8
Is It a Fact that Facts Don't Matter?

DAVID RAMSAY STEELE

Facts don't matter, or so Scott Adams keeps telling us.

This looks like an outrageous claim. He sometimes qualifies it by saying that "Facts matter for outcomes but not for persuasion" and sometimes seems to back away from it by saying that "Facts are over-rated" (implying they do matter at least a little bit).

And despite his flat assertion that facts don't matter, Scott spends much of his time on his blog and on Periscope disputing matters of fact. He tells us that he was one of the few to predict Trump's victory—he assures us that this is a *fact*, and that *it matters a lot*. More generally, he tells us that Persuasion is "a good filter because it predicts well"—he tells us that this is a *fact*, and that it *matters a lot*. And of course he repeatedly informs us that "facts don't matter," which if true must be a *fact that matters a lot* (and that would be a *performative contradiction*, but hey, Scott's impatient with technicalities so we'll steer clear of them).

In fact, Scott can't talk for five minutes or write for two pages without making his argument depend on matters of fact which really do matter for his argument. So how can it possibly be that facts don't matter?

Well, maybe he thinks that facts don't matter for most people, though they quite obviously do matter to him? Or maybe we can make some sense of his strange claim that "facts matter for outcomes but not for persuasion"? Or perhaps he means only that politicians sometimes win elections despite making a lot of factually inaccurate claims? Or perhaps he's practicing what he sees as Donald Trump's "anchor" strategy—making a seemingly outlandish claim to attract attention and situate the negotiation, a claim which he will later dial back to a more moderate statement?

The Two Meanings of "Facts"

What are facts? Dictionaries give several alternative (and sometimes incompatible) definitions of the word "fact." However, these alternative definitions can be grouped into two basic ideas:

1. **"Facts" are the way things really are (or were), independent of what anyone thinks.**

2. **"Facts" are statements which have been certified as true, either by common consent or by some authority, such as a consensus of experts.**

It can be confusing that there are these two common uses of the word "fact," as they are often contrary in meaning. In sense #1, it's possible for everyone to be wrong about a fact, or just to be totally unaware of it, whereas in sense #2, nothing can be a fact until someone has become aware of it and considered it to be a fact.

A little thought shows, in fact, that the vast majority of facts in sense #1 can never be known by anyone—for example, think about such facts as the precise configuration of molecules inside a distant star, or how many beans were in that can I opened a year ago. The universe contains an infinity of facts in sense #1, and very nearly all of them are forever unknowable.

Furthermore a fact in sense #2 may not be a fact in sense #1, because common consent or the judgments of experts may be mistaken. Facts in sense #2 sometimes change. It used to be a "fact" in sense #2 that continents do not move, that homosexuality is a mental illness, and that it's hazardous to your health to go swimming immediately after a meal. None of these are "facts" in sense #2 any longer.

Assuming that we've now got these facts right, then the sense #2 facts we now possess always were sense #1 facts, and the older sense #2 facts were never sense #1 facts, though people thought they were. Sense #1 facts never change, as long as we stipulate the date—a sense #1 fact may stop being a fact at a point in time, but then it's still a fact that this fact was a fact before that point in time.

Although the two senses are sometimes opposed to each other, there is an intimate connection between them. We're concerned about sense #2 facts because we think that they're generally likely to give us sense #1 facts, at least a lot of the time. If we thought that a sense #2 fact had only a fifty-fifty chance of being a sense #1 fact, we would lose interest in sense #2 facts.

Confusion may arise if we don't keep the distinction clear between sense #1 and sense #2. When Kellyanne Conway said that she would look for some "alternative facts," this became viral and was taken by many to imply that she thought we could pick and choose our reality, like O'Brien in *Nineteen Eighty-Four*. But close attention to that actual exchange between Kellyanne and Chuck Todd, and the other comments by President Trump and Sean Spicer, reveals that Kellyanne, Sean, and the president were very definitely talking about sense #2 facts. They weren't disputing for a moment that sense #1 facts are objective and independent of what anyone believes, though in this particular disputed case, whether Trump's Inaugural crowd was bigger than Obama's, it looks to me that the Trump people were probably sincerely mistaken.

The attribution to Trump and his supporters of the view that facts in sense #1 can be chosen at will is not only wrong (not a fact); it's extremely weird, because there are indeed a lot of people who deny the objectivity or absoluteness of truth (post-modernists, social constructivists, anti-realists, and truth-relativists) and these people are all on the left. This is a characteristic belief of leftist intellectuals, and is never found on today's right.

David Ramsay Steele

Cognitive Dissonance

Scott talks a lot about "Cognitive Dissonance," a concept which plays a big role in his theory of how people form their ideas. In *Win Bigly* (p. 48), he introduces Cognitive Dissonance by citing the Wikipedia definition. The basic idea is that Cognitive Dissonance is the discomfort or mental stress people have when they find a conflict between one thing they believe and something else they have come to believe.

The first thing to notice here is that this phenomenon of Cognitive Dissonance does not arise in most everyday cases where we find we have been mistaken. I was sure I had left my keys on the coffee table, but when I look, they're not there. I start to search in the other likely places, and soon find them in my coat pocket. I had made a mistake; my memory was slightly faulty; no big deal. I'm not distressed. People revise their beliefs and acknowledge their mistakes all the time. Scott is demonstrably wrong when he says that Cognitive Dissonance "often" happens in "daily experience." It almost never happens in daily experience.

But there certainly are cases (a small minority of cases) where a major assumption is challenged by events, leading to emotional distress and sometimes to the production of what Scott calls "hallucinations," highly fanciful stories which reconcile the person's prior assumption with what has unexpectedly happened. Scott, in fact, soon forgets the Wikipedia definition and then begins to use his own definition of Cognitive Dissonance, in which "your brain automatically generates an illusion to solve the discomfort" (pp. 48–49).

So, for Scott, the crux of Cognitive Dissonance is an illusion. This presupposes a distinction between illusion and reality, and therefore presupposes that *facts matter a whole darn freaking lot*. Exhibit A for Scott's argument is, of course, the election of Donald Trump on November 8th 2016. Many people had thought the election of Trump, though an appalling hypothetical, was practically impossible, but it happened, and so these people experienced mental discomfort, and some of them began to believe very fanciful stories.

As Scott reminds us, these "hallucinations" (a term he extends to include any belief in tall tales) are more common among the party out of power. In the time of Obama, some Republican voters believed that Obama was a Muslim, while in the time of Trump some Democratic voters believed that Trump had "colluded with the Russians."

When we look at these exceptional cases of what Scott calls "Cognitive Dissonance," what do we see?

The first thing we notice is that this Cognitive Dissonance is brought about by the realization that something is seriously wrong: we find ourselves inclined to believe in two things which can't both be true, and we know that this can't be right. Sometimes, as with the election of Donald Trump to the presidency, the contradiction arises because we have to accept that something has happened which our prior beliefs implied could not happen.

A standard example would be a religious sect which preaches that the world is going to end on a particular day. That day comes and goes without any obvious disruption, and the sect has to decide what to make of this—they may begin to preach that the world did end on that date, despite superficial appearances, or they may conclude they got their calculations wrong, and fix on a new, future date when the world will end.

The awareness that something is seriously wrong arises because of our acceptance of facts. What it shows is that *facts are tremendously important*. Facts matter more than *almost* anything else could possibly matter! There is (as a matter of fact) just one thing—only one!—that matters more than facts, and I'll tell you what it is in a moment.

Without our acceptance of facts, this Cognitive Dissonance could not arise. It's only because we accept that Trump did in fact become president-elect that we perceive a clash between this acceptance and our prior theory which told us it could not happen. This Cognitive Dissonance also requires that we recognize the law of logic which states that we can't simultaneously accept a statement and its negation. So, we can't accept that "Trump was elected president" and "Trump was not elected president." The understanding that elementary logic is supreme is innate in all competent humans, in all cultures and social classes, at all historical times.

When we come up with what Scott calls an "illusion" to reconcile the new facts with our prevailing assumptions, what we're doing is to accept the newly discovered facts while trying to preserve as much of our prevailing assumptions as we can, without self-contradiction, especially those assumptions we see as most fundamental. *This is a rational response.*

Coming to Terms with the Reality of Trump

After Trump had been elected but before the Inauguration, Scott predicted that Trump's opponents in the first year of the Trump presidency would go through the following stages:

1. They would at first say that "Trump is Hitler."

2. About halfway through the year, they would concede that Trump is not Hitler, but would say he was incompetent, perhaps even crazy.

3. By the end of the year, they would concede he was highly competent and therefore effective, but would assert that they didn't like his policies.

Scott is justly very proud of this series of predictions, which have broadly come true (though he didn't foresee the eruption of the "Russian collusion" story, nor did he foresee the brief revival of the "Trump is crazy" theory following the release of Michael Wolff's book *Fire and Fury* in January 2018). Scott's latest prediction is that people will soon start talking about America's new "Golden Age."

However, as Scott's account makes clear (but Scott himself apparently doesn't notice), the fulfillment of these predictions depended on *the over-arching importance of brute facts*. According to Scott's account:

1. The disappearance of the claim that Trump is Hitler results from unavoidable awareness of the *fact* that Trump has not done any Hitler-like things.

2. The disappearance of the claim that Trump is incompetent results from unavoidable awareness of the *fact* that he accomplished more than most presidents in his first year.

By Scott's own account, then, in these two cases, the facts are absolutely decisive. He just takes for granted, without any hesitation, that people had no alternative but to acknowledge these facts.

When Trump was elected, we can imagine the anti-Trump believers "hallucinating" that Hillary had been declared winner, that Trump had conceded, that Hillary gave the Inaugural Address on 20th January 2017, and that Hillary was now in the Oval Office, carrying out the duties of president, no doubt superbly. But not one of the millions of Hillary supporters reacted in this way. Quite the opposite, they wept and wailed, bemoaning the undeniable fact that Hillary had lost the election. Clearly, *facts are sometimes decisive*, according to Scott's own account.

Another way the Hillary supporters could have failed to accept the demonstrated fact of Trump's election victory would have been to "hallucinate" that on November 8th 2016 the world was occupied by space aliens who abolished the United States of America along with its constitution and election procedures. These space aliens now directly governed what had been the US and we all became subject to their edicts. Not one of the millions of Hillary supporters opted for that theory!

Why did all the millions of Hillary supporters, without exception, fail to adopt one of these theories, or any of numerous other fanciful yarns we could dream up? *According to Scott's own account,* there was just one explanation for this: all these millions of people had to accept the facts. *The facts were irresistible.*

Having accepted the unwelcome *fact* that Trump was now president, the Hillary supporters responded to this unwelcome *fact* by claiming that Trump was Hitler. Although inaccurate, this was not entirely arbitrary. It was essentially a continuation of what many of them had been saying before the election. They had been saying that if you elected Trump you would be electing Hitler. No doubt to some of them this was hyperbole, but they didn't mind taking the risk that many others would interpret it literally, and now they found themselves hoist by their own hyperbole.

As the months went by, Trump failed to do anything remotely like Hitler. He did not set up concentration camps, outlaw all political parties except his own, murder his critics or rivals, or act in any way outside the previously existing law. He criticized Obama for having usurped the legislative role of Congress, complied with the decisions of courts, and did not propose that judicial review should be abolished. Nor did he grow a mustache.

The involuntary acceptance of facts caused changes in ideas. We can easily imagine that the Hillary supporters might have "hallucinated" that concentration camps were under construction, that all political parties except the Republicans had been outlawed, that Hillary, Bill, Barack, Michelle, Elizabeth Warren, John McCain, and Michael Moore had been assassinated in a "June Purge." *But not one of the Hillary supporters reacted like this.* Instead, they all accepted that Trump was not Hitler after all, and moved on to the theory that he was "incompetent" or even "crazy" and that the White House was "in chaos."

This was also factually inaccurate, but again, it was not entirely arbitrary. It returned to charges made against Trump during the election campaign. Trump's decisive management style, his plebeian bluntness of speech, and his readiness to let people go who hadn't worked out could easily be represented as someone just flailing around. His tweets could be described as impulsive, ill-considered responses to immediate provocations. It took a while before perceptive people, with the help of Scott Adams, came to understand that the Trump tweets were essentially strategic and adroitly crafted: Trump was counterbalancing the hostile propaganda pouring out from CNN and MSNBC; he was reaching a hundred million followers several times a day, and he was doing so (as he occasionally pointed out) for free.

The "incompetent or crazy" theory was killed by the demonstrable fact that Trump was effective; more than most presidents he was getting things done. Of course, we may not *like* some of the things he was getting done (and when it comes to the Wall, protective tariffs, and the wars in Syria and Afghanistan, I don't), but, as Scott rightly insists, that's a separate matter. More than half the country does like them.

Notice that, once again, acceptance of the fact that Trump was fully competent was involuntary. It was thrust upon the reluctant Hillary supporters by factual evidence that could hardly be contested, culminating in the successful passage of the Tax Cuts and Jobs Bill in December 2017, which all experienced observers attributed in large part to Trump's management skills and capacity for hard work. By the time Trump achieved a rare perfect score on a standard test of cognitive ability, most people had already abandoned the theory that he was incompetent.

What Kind of a Genius?

Scott tells us that Trump is a Master Persuader. He goes so far as to claim that Trump could have taken a different policy agenda and won with it, because of his persuasive skills (*Win Bigly*, pp. 92–93). He even says Trump could have won by persuasion if his and Hillary's policies were simply switched.

While Trump's persuasive skills are certainly extraordinary, and Scott has helped me and thousands of others to appreciate that, I believe we can explain Trump's political success differently, and I very much doubt that Trump could have won with a substantially different agenda. I believe his choice of agenda was part of a shrewdly calculated political strategy. A linchpin of this strategy is the traditional working class in the Rust Belt states. These people had seen their real wages reduced, they had seen mining and manufacturing decimated as companies moved offshore, and they had seen that the Democratic Party would do nothing for them, not even to the extent of paying lip-service to their interests or having candidates visit their neighborhoods.

Trump, Hillary, and the Issues

In the 2016 election campaign, Trump constantly hammered away at the issues, while Hillary ran away from the issues. This was obvious to all those who followed the speeches and the TV ads on both sides, but if anyone had any doubts, there was a scholarly study of precisely this point, conducted in March 2017 by the Wesleyan Media Project. This study corroborated what was evident to anyone who followed both sides of the campaign.

All of Trump's many rally speeches were densely focused on the policies he advocated. Only briefly would he make a nasty remark about Hillary's personality or past misdeeds, then he would swiftly return to his advocacy of very specific policies. The same was even more true of the TV ads for Trump. On Hillary's side, both speeches and TV ads gave very little attention to policy issues—far less than any other presidential candidate in living memory—and put all the emphasis on Trump's horrible and frightening personality. As the Wesleyan study cautiously put it, "Clinton's message was devoid of policy discussions in a way not seen in the previous four presidential contests."

Trump's rally speeches never wandered far from the specific issues, so that anyone following the campaign even casually became acutely conscious of Trump's policy proposals, whereas most voters had little idea of Clinton's policies. Trump made many commitments, broad and narrow, about tightening up immigration, whereas Clinton rarely spelled out her own policy on immigration, and most voters had no idea what it was. Voters might assume that Clinton favored doing nothing to change immigration controls or even that she favored moving to "open borders." Dedicated policy wonks might be able to ascertain that actually Clinton also favored tightening up immigration controls, though *perhaps* slightly less severely than Trump, but voters who merely watched the news would never have guessed this.

It's clear that Clinton just could not talk too much about immigration policy, for this would be to concede, in effect, that she shared a lot of common ground with Obama and with Trump. She could hardly boast about the steep increase in deportations of aliens under Obama, while denouncing Trump for his proposed deportations, much less could she promise voters that deportations would be accelerated once she was in the Oval Office. That would tend to go against the claim that Trump was uniquely evil for wanting to deport aliens. For similar reasons, she could hardly brag about Obama's facilitation of oil and gas pipelines and promise to continue or escalate this policy.

There has probably never been a previous election in American history where one candidate's numerous policy proposals have been so familiar to the general electorate, while the other candidate's proposals were almost unknown. Clinton based everything on the proposition that she was personally superior to Trump—more specifically that Trump was a monster and at least fifty percent of his supporters (she meant a quarter of the population, the working class) were "deplorable" monsters.

Everyone who followed the campaign, even superficially, would know that Trump was advocating:

1. **A tightening up of controls on immigration, especially more effective enforcement of existing laws restricting immigration.**

2. **Repeal or renegotiation of trade agreements such as NAFTA and TPP.**

3. **Revival of manufacturing in the Rust Belt, partly because of #2 but also because of targeted protectionist measures such as penalties for companies which opened up plant**

abroad, tariffs on imports, and a general government policy of "Buy American, Hire American."

4. Defense of the Second Amendment—Americans' constitutional right to own and carry guns.

5. Appointment of conservative judges who would follow the
   Original Intent of the Constitution.

6. A "pro-life" stance which in effect meant giving abortion
   policy back to the democratic process in the states, rather
   than a court-imposed "pro-choice" policy.

7. Repeal and replacement of Obamacare.

8. Abstention from wars (like Iraq and Libya) which don't
   yield any net benefit to the US.

9. Major reforms in the treatment of veterans.

10. Increased military spending.

11. A major drive to repair and modernize infrastructure.

Everybody knows that these were Trump's policies. Now,
quick, what was Hillary's policy on each of these issues? You
see? You don't have the foggiest notion. You might guess that
she would keep Obamacare, though she said she would overhaul it, and in politics the line between overhaul and replacement is fuzzy.

Trump vacillated between extreme and moderate versions of these policies, but he never reversed them during
the campaign. What was, in effect, Clinton's reply to these
proposals? First, Trump is an evil person and we are not
Trump. Second, we are entitled to be president because we
are a woman. However, according to Clinton's leftist supporters, anyone who decides to be a woman becomes a woman,
and therefore Trump could at any time become the first
woman president simply by announcing "I'm a woman!"

Most of the time, Clinton avoided responding to Trump's
policy proposals with her own. She did her best to avoid any
comparison of the opposing policies, and to keep the focus on

Trump's personality, a risky strategy as many people found her own personality unendearing and her own past conduct questionable. But don't forget that if she had won, this strategy would have been hailed as awesomely clever.

The thing that most caused me to rapidly revise my very dismissive view of Trump shortly after the election was not just that he won, but that he won in precisely the way he said he would win. He knew what he was doing; he had better intelligence about the voters. TV interviews with personnel of his polling firm, Cambridge Analytica, corroborated this interpretation.

My guess is that Trump, years before the election, had already seen that a dramatic comeback for American manufacturing and mining was inevitable—indeed, was already in its early stages—alongside the ignorant conventional view that manufacturing and mining were in permanent decline. He could therefore not only make political capital from the plight of the Rust Belt but also, once elected, ride the wave of manufacturing and mining revival. In business circles, people were already talking about "reshoring"—the phenomenon of companies bringing their plant back into the United States. This talk originated at the beginning of the century but had mostly still not trickled down into the popular media, and now it is doing so it will be difficult to separate from the achievements of Trump, especially as Trump has admittedly done a number of things to give it a boost.

The inevitable comeback for American manufacturing was a commonplace among business analysts years before the election (see for instance the 2012 study, *The US Manufacturing Renaissance: How Shifting Global Economics Are Creating an American Comeback*). Reshoring has several causes, including the spectacular and continuing rise of Chinese wages and the development of fracking, which guarantees amazingly cheap American energy for many generations to come. During the campaign, anti-Trump commentators often showed their ignorance by proclaiming that the decline of manufacturing and mining were irreversible, even as both were already rebounding robustly.

Obama did occasionally try to explain what was going on, but the one line that resonated was "Some of these jobs are just not going to come back." Oops. There go several thousand Michigan votes. And Hillary: "Because we're going to put a lot of coal miners and coal companies out of business, right?" Oh, dear. There go several thousand Pennsylvania and West Virginia votes. The fact that these lines were taken out of context and hurt the Democratic campaign shows that there is cunning in Trump's apparent crudeness in making bold assertions and almost never qualifying them.

The Obama administration officially began measures to promote reshoring in 2011, but Hillary didn't make much of this during the campaign. This was in keeping with her avoidance of policy talk and her haughty disdain for the working class, those dumb rednecks, who, just like Blacks and Hispanics, could be relied upon to vote Democratic without being offered any serious incentive to do so. And while Hillary knew enough to understand that fracking is a tremendous boon to humanity and a guarantee of economic growth, she was no doubt afraid to drive voters to Bernie Sanders and then to Jill Stein by enthusiastically embracing cheap energy, underwritten by fracking. Obama had celebrated fracking but Hillary didn't dare to do so.

A general theme of Clintonism is that it relied on harnessing the energies of leftists while favoring ruling-class privilege. Hillary was embarrassed by any shining of the light on specific policies, because she wanted both the votes and the activist work of "progressives" and the financial donations of "neo-liberals" and "globalists," and she feared that frank talk about specifics could only scare away one or the other.

Scott occasionally mentions Hillary's discussions of "policy details" (p. 164), implying that this was a boring and fact-oriented preoccupation by contrast with Trump's nebulous and exciting "Persuasion." Nothing could be further from the truth. The Hillary campaign was simply astounding and unprecedented in its avoidance of any talk about policies, as the Wesleyan study proves. As far as most voters could tell,

Hillary had just one policy: hatred for Trump's personality. This avoidance of policy issues is connected with another feature of the Hillary campaign, familiar from the book *Shattered*. Hillary never came up with a story as to why she was running. Trump was running to "Make America Great Again," and he would sometimes unpack it: "Make America Rich Again, Make America Strong Again, Make America Safe Again"—tightly linked to all the eleven policy proposals mentioned above.

The Democrats made things worse for themselves by talking about Trump's appeal to the "white working class." Plenty of Blacks and Hispanics had lost manufacturing jobs in the Rust Belt. Trump picked up unexpected Black, Hispanic, and Muslim votes, and among white workers he did especially well with former Obama and Sanders voters, beginning his long-term plan of permanently detaching the working class of all races from the Democratic Party.

Trump plays a long game. A tightening of immigration controls is popular with voters, including those Hispanics and Muslims who are already here legally. Purely from the standpoint of political opportunism, what's even better than being elected to tighten up immigration controls and then doing so? What's better is being publicly opposed at every step in struggling to tighten up immigration controls. This continually reminds voters that there are forces at work plotting to frustrate the president and the popular will, and therefore constantly broadcasts the urgency of continuing to support the president. The Sanctuary City–Sanctuary State movement might have been engineered to guarantee Trump's re-election by a landslide in 2020.

Trump finds issues where the majority is on his side, and where he's therefore likely to win in the long term, yet where he has to visibly battle against opposition. Even before he won in 2016—and he knew he was going to win—he was thinking of how he would manage his first term to ensure his re-election in 2020. As I have learned from my own earlier blunders in this area, the biggest mistake you can make about Trump is to suppose that he *ever* acts on impulse.

Trump is a supremely self-controlled person who always acts methodically according to a long-range plan. Ignore this fact, and you may already have lost against Trump.

"People Are Not Rational"

As Scott repeatedly tells us, his contention that facts don't matter arises from his fundamental conviction that people are not rational. According to Scott, "humans are not rational. We bounce from one illusion to another, all the while thinking we are seeing something we call reality" (*Win Bigly*, p. 37).

The theory that people are fundamentally irrational is the fashionable one. We are constantly bombarded by books and articles from a wide range of sources telling us that people don't make decisions rationally but emotionally, and then invent false reasons for why they decided the way they did.

However, as we've seen, when Scott is not intoning the fashionable dogma that people are irrational, he keeps forgetting it, and keeps reminding us, unintentionally, that people do change their beliefs in accordance with facts and logic.

So what about the rare exceptional cases which Scott calls "Cognitive Dissonance"? What about the theory held by Hillary supporters in January through June 2017 that Trump was Hitler? Or the theory held after June 2017 that Trump was incompetent or crazy?

Though both these beliefs were seriously mistaken, I wouldn't call them irrational. The view that humans are rational doesn't require that they never make mistakes—quite the contrary: only a rational being can make a mistake.

So, can I defend the "hallucinations" of Cognitive Dissonance as rational? I believe I can. The first thing to note is that such illusions are generally short-lived. Scott's ideas about Persuasion focus on the short-range and the short-term. Theories about Trump as Hitler or Trump as mentally defective, as well as theories about "Russian collusion," have now largely evaporated.

What happens when something occurs that people's previous ideas had been telling them could not possibly occur?

They adjust their previous ideas, and their first stab at adjusting their ideas may not be the long-range adjustment.

Karl Popper has explained how people develop their ideas through conjecture and refutation, in other words by making unjustified guesses and then disproving those guesses, and moving on to new and better (but still unjustified) guesses. That's how human rationality works. That's the only way it could work. That's what happens in the examples offered by Scott.

Can We Handle the Truth?

A recurring theme in Scott's writing and speaking is that we're not equipped to get at the truth. Remarks like this are scattered throughout his written and oral output: "The human brain is not capable of comprehending truth at a deep level" (p. 28).

Scott often talks about the fact that people of different opinions can be watching "two movies on the same screen." Another metaphor he uses is that of "filters." He says that he prefers to use the "Persuasion" filter, while other people may use other filters.

But can't we say that one movie or filter is to be preferred to another because it is more accurate? Here Scott equivocates. At times he implies that any such preference is a matter of taste. But, naturally, he doesn't want to let go of the notion that his Persuasion movie or filter has something to recommend it! If he did that, there would be no reason to pay any attention to his arguments.

What Scott repeatedly says is that we can never really know the truth, but we can prefer one "movie" or "filter" to another because

1. **It makes us happy and**

2. **It is predictive.**

So, Scott argues, we adopt a point of view not because we think it's true, but because it makes us happy to think about it and it gives us good predictions (pp. 38–47).

But if a theory (what Scott calls a "filter") makes us happy and makes good predictions, is that so different from being true? These are not exactly the same, but they do seem to overlap quite a bit—especially because a theory most often makes us "happy" by making sense to us, by striking us as a reasonable explanation. So, if someone had said in 2015 that a powerful coven of witches in Kazakhstan had cast a spell to ensure that Trump would win the Republican Party nomination and go on to win the US presidency, this would have been predictive, but would not have made us "happy," only because we don't believe that witches can influence the outcome of elections by casting spells.

What makes us happy is largely a matter of our existing theories about the world. A new theory tends to make us happy when it fits with the totality of our existing theories—and this, I claim, is perfectly rational (though, of course, not infallible).

As well as Cognitive Dissonance, Scott talks a lot about Confirmation Bias. He sees this as an example of irrationality. But confirmation bias is rational! As Karl Popper pointed out, our theories would be useless if we gave them up too easily. If the power goes out in my apartment, I don't immediately abandon my belief in Coulomb's Law or Ohm's Law. I automatically save my most fundamental beliefs and give up more minor beliefs: in this case, my belief that the fuses were not overloaded.

While facts do matter, *theories matter more*. Our preconceived assumptions—our theories—tend to dominate our thinking, *and that's rational*, but sometimes these theories can be tested against facts, and sometimes the facts are decisive in causing us to change our theories. That's rational too.

If facts matter and theories matter, what about Scott's exalted idea of persuasion? Everyone knows that persuasion can have some independent effect. Philosophers have always known that persuasion has a role, complementary to theories and facts. Two and half thousand years ago, Aristotle wrote a textbook of logic, his *Prior Analytics*. He also wrote a textbook of persuasion, his *Rhetoric*.

Is It a Fact that Facts Don't Matter?

As Ray Scott Percival has argued (in *The Myth of the Closed Mind*), persuasion, advertising, and propaganda can all be explained within the theory that humans are rational. Here I will just throw out one hint. When he claims that "facts don't matter" and that "people are irrational," Scott always focuses his attention on the very short run. He looks at people's *immediate* responses to "Cognitive Dissonance." When he considers events lasting more than a few months, he always, *in practice* though not explicitly, acknowledges that facts can be decisive and usually are.

Election campaigns are comparatively brief events which take place within a framework of prevailing ideas that can't be challenged without political loss, and these ideas are often the outcome of influences working slowly over decades or centuries. For example, who was the first newly elected US president to be openly in favor of gay marriage? The answer (surprising to some) is: Donald J. Trump. When Barack Obama was elected in 2008, he presented himself as a most emphatic and deeply committed opponent of gay marriage. If he had come out in favor of gay marriage in that year, it would have been too risky.

Between 2008 and 2016, public opinion changed so that it became more of an electoral liability than an advantage to oppose gay marriage. And this change was itself the culmination of slow changes in opinion over many decades.

One thing that follows from this is that if you want to influence people's political thinking for years ahead, you probably won't want to become too involved in election campaigns.

9
But Women Can Vote . . .

Sandra Hansmann and Cynthia Jones

As the one female main character in *Dilbert*, Alice is smart, but angry and violent. Now we could be wrong, but she sounds a bit like an "angry feminist." And then there's Carol, Dilmom, and Tina, none of whom are particularly flattering portrayals of women, but hey, it's a cartoon, and no one in *Dilbert*, except maybe Dilbert, is a hero.

There aren't many females in *Dilbert*, but males are still the norm in engineering and IT, so fair enough. But we might still wonder about Scott Adams's views on gender and women. We needn't wonder too much, however, as Adams is a prolific blogger who has made a number of interesting pronouncements on these topics.

The Waves of Feminism

The wave metaphor is employed in describing historical trends in feminism on the assumption that interest in women's rights and specific issues reaches a peak and then falls off. The first wave of feminism was predominantly about political rights and voting rights for women. Remember that women, as half the population in our country, didn't "gain" the right to vote in the US until 1920.

A few decades later, the second wave of feminism gathered momentum when feminists like Simone de Beauvoir in her seminal work *The Second Sex* made explicit the historical and contemporary oppression of women, demonstrating that the right to vote hadn't come close to changing the balance of power between men and women. The third wave of feminism focused on the lack of attention paid to issues of race and economics, arguing that oppression looks very different based on race, ethnicity, and economics, while arguing that the intersectionality of different versions of oppression had been ignored by previous feminisms, as had the voices of women of color. The fourth wave of feminism is characterized by activism surrounding issues of sexual harassment and violence against women and is tied to the use of social media to disseminate information and create a space for new and perhaps marginalized voices to be heard.

Cartoon by Julietta Rivera

But what is the so-called men's rights movement and why has it, and Scott Adams, pissed off so many people in its defense?

But What about Men?

The men's rights movement—which, like most movements is multifaceted and encompasses several different sub-groups— developed in the 1960s and 1970s as both a parallel movement of and a response to second- and third-wave feminism. By the 1990s, the men's rights movement and men's rights activists has distilled their platform into a fairly distinct slate of issues including specific concerns about issues of due process and unequal legal treatment under the law to more nebulous and malicious complaints about feminisms and the destruction of the patriarchy. The party line of men's rights activists is typified by a disproportionate sense of discrimination, entitlement, victimization, and in many cases, outright misogyny.

Scott Adams stepped into the morass that is the men's rights movement in March 2011 on his personal blog (http://blog.dilbert.com), with a reader-requested post titled simply, "Men's Rights." He insisted the post was intended to skewer the men's rights movement and men's rights activists, which he did. Nonetheless, his treatment of women was far more negative because, as he opined, traditional masculinity is both the problem and the solution.

In addressing men's rights activists, Adams says to such men in his March 2011 post:

> Get over it, you bunch of pussies.
> The reality is that women are treated differently by society for exactly the same reason that children and the mentally handicapped are treated differently. It's just easier this way for everyone. You don't argue with a four-year-old about why he shouldn't eat candy for dinner. You don't punch a mentally handicapped guy even if he punches you first. And you don't argue when a women tells you she's only making 80 cents to your dollar. It's the path of least resistance. You save your energy for more important battles.

Leaving aside the incredibly problematic insult to the men's rights activists by calling them "pussies" (why is a pussy a weak thing, by the way?), which we assume was done to be particularly insulting to the manly men typifying the men's rights movement, this blog post has been reposted and attacked and defended a myriad of times. Adams himself attempts to shame the hysterical feminists who take this piece out of context, like we have here, and makes it clear that they (the hysterical and angry feminists) are not his target audience as they lack the depth to understand his humor (March 25th 2011 post).

> This piece was designed for regular readers of The Scott Adams blog. That group has an unusually high reading comprehension level.
> In this case, the content of the piece inspires so much emotion in some readers that they literally can't understand it. The same

would be true if the topic were about gun ownership or a dozen other topics. As emotion increases, reading comprehension decreases. This would be true of anyone, but regular readers of the Dilbert blog are pretty far along the bell curve toward rational thought, and relatively immune to emotional distortion.

Adding insult to injury, Adam's post was no one-off. Following up on this initial 2011 controversy, he has gone on to author a number of other men's-right's-movement-supporting blog posts. These posts suggest an affinity with men's rights activists rather deeper than he claims or perhaps even recognizes, particularly in his examinations of key feminist issues across various waves of feminism.

Women as Children

A significant recurring theme on many men's rights activist websites is that of the unreliable female narrator—women simply don't know or understand their own lives, and dissemble (intentionally or unintentionally) about everything from the salary gap to rape. This rhetoric is an eerie echo of the rhetoric of a number of early anti-suffragists, including Mrs. William Force Scott and Senator J.B. Sanford, both of whom argued variously that women were too flighty, too delicate, and—especially in the case of poorer, less educated women—too ignorant to vote.

From the perspective of the modern men's rights movement, similar rhetoric describes women as "flaky," spoiled, unreasonable, or wheedling, and justifies not only the value but also the need for men's elevated position relative to women and other social (as opposed to racial) minorities. Some authors have termed this position "familial" patriarchy in which manliness is the strongly preferred state, while women are positioned alongside their toddlers as individuals who can't be trusted to act in their own best interests, much less run the world.

Scott Adams neatly encapsulates the sentiment by lumping women, children, and the mentally handicapped together; espousing alignment with this particular area of the men's rights movement when he noted that "women are treated differently by society for exactly the same reason that children and the mentally handicapped are treated differently. It's just easier this way for everyone . . ."

Although Adams attempted later to qualify this comment, he in fact doubled down, noting that the ways men must deal with these three groups is "disturbingly similar" and the best (and perhaps only) coping strategy for men is to remember not to care when those who are less-competent start to whine. Surely the anti-suffragettes themselves would have approved.

The Voting Matriarchy

In recent years, the men's rights movement has focused with growing zeal on the perceived toxic consequences of feminism as a force that frees women from male control at societal and personal levels and thus threatens the status quo—the patriarchy. Men's rights activists believe a transfer of rights and power from the boys to the girls has occurred, and so we're now living in a matriarchy. However, most modern anthropologists consider "matriarchy" a myth; there is no known (not myth-based) society, past or present, in which women truly ruled. Nonetheless, many men's rights activists consider any societal system not wholly grounded in traditional masculine interests to be a de facto matriarchy, though of course no serious scholars share this view.

But for Scott Adams, the notation of a female-dominated matriarchal United States is quite real. In his "Global Gender War" post from 2015, Adams gives us his definition: matriarchies are female-dominated countries, and female-dominated countries are those in which women can vote.

I wonder if the discussion of so-called radical Islam is disguising the fact that male-dominated societies are at war with female-dominated countries. Correct me if I'm wrong, but Islam doesn't look so dangerous in countries where women can vote. Consider the United States . . . compare our matriarchy (that we pretend is a patriarchy) with the situation in DAESH-held territory. That's what a male-dominated society looks like.

Adams expands this line of reasoning to a global context, noting that worldwide, male-dominated societies are at war with female-dominated countries as a way of explaining the tensions between the West and Middle East. Troublingly, Adams writes without any sense of knowledge or awareness that women are grievously oppressed in the Middle Eastern countries he's referencing, despite having gained their voting rights much earlier than American women. Clearly, gaining the right to vote is just a small step to actual political power.

Somehow, despite their matriarchal power, women still have certain (mostly sexual) obligations to men. According to Adams, the result is that our female-dominated society has evolved to keep men constantly unfulfilled and unhappy. He has dedicated quite a bit of blog space to the issue of matriarchy, noting that typically feminine behavior is valued, while masculine behaviors outside of a few exceptions in sports and war are stifled. Like most members of the men's rights movement, he blames women for this state of affairs—they have men by the balls for sure, forcing them to wear V-neck sweaters (blog post from June 23rd 2016). He encourages women to put down their feminist sledgehammers—surely, since you can vote, it's time to relax ladies! But since feminist relaxation is unlikely to happen, how does Scott Adams propose to deal with the new matriarchal order inside the US? Why, just give up and submit to chemical castration (blog post from June 15th 2011).

Men's Entitlement to Women's Bodies

Women's control over their own bodies, especially in the area of reproductive control, was a central issue of second-wave feminism, and one to which the men's rights movement continues to respond vociferously. More recently, bodily integrity has become a central concern in fourth-wave feminism with the emergence of #metoo and similar anti-sexual harassment and assault movements.

All of these concepts trouble the men's rights movement greatly, since in varying ways, they all challenge men's sexual entitlement to women's bodies and men's power to control the narrative about that entitlement. Only a cursory review of the most popular men's rights movement websites is needed to demonstrate the growing pushback among men's rights activists about anti-rape efforts and sexual consent standards. Many groups cast the concept of rape culture as a feminist moral panic, although they are usually careful to couch the conversation in terms of political correctness run amok. For some men's rights activists, these concerns have evolved into a clear preoccupation with false claims of sexual violence.

As Scott Adams and men's rights activists see it, the matriarchy not only exists, it exists as a prison for men's desires, forcing them to their knees in their relationships and interfering with their entitlement to women's attention, love, and bodies. Almost all men's rights movement websites demonstrate this sense of entitlement, although in different and differently upsetting ways. Many men's rights activists see themselves as natural pursuers/horn dogs and access to sex as a biological right, a stance that Scott Adams certainly seems to support. He has noted (post from March 27th 2011) that men have natural instincts for sex and aggression, and only suppress them as a strategy to have an even better sexual outcome later.

> How many times do we men suppress our natural instincts for sex and aggression just to get something better in the long run? It's called a strategy. Sometimes you sacrifice a pawn to nail the queen.

Likewise, women grant or withhold access to sex as a means to some end—usually financial or relational, another common theme of men's rights activists—to either men's delight or frustration. A number of men's rights movement groups endorse the notion that sexual frustration leads to rape. If women were just less stingy with blowjobs, they argue, surely rape rates would go down. As objectionable as that view seems, Scott Adams has actually gone further, suggesting that sexual frustration is linked not only to rape but also to murder in the form of ISIS/Daesh suicide bombings, when he suggests that in the absence of 'hugging' it's logical and perhaps even biological to turn to killing instead (blog post from November 17th 2015).

Women as Shrews

While first-wave feminism focused on participation of women in the political sphere, the second wave focused more on broader equality in society, especially in the world of work. But in both eras, the opposition rolled out similar gender stereotypes grounded in domesticity, employing images and narratives of women behaving in un-ladylike, un-motherly ways to shame them into compliance with social norms.

This form of opposition continues today, and while almost all men's rights movement groups engage in various forms of gender stereotyping, the current stereotype of women as unfeminine shrews is particularly insidious. Men's rights activists often contend that feminism overall, and our matriarchal system specifically, educates and encourages women to henpeck and manipulate men. Casting women as verbose, emotional, and irrational beings gives men permission to ignore them.

Taking that train of thought a bit further, it's not unusual for men's rights activists to see traditionalist women as gold diggers intent on trapping men into marriage and the care of children. These harpies are intent on male humiliation and emasculation. On the other hand, they see feminist women as gold diggers of a different sort, intent on snagging men's jobs through double-talk, manipulation, sex, or promises of sex. These harpies are intent on humiliating and emasculating men. Researchers have labeled this peculiarly men's rights movement phenomenon the "Goldilocks

Dilemma" because for many of them the modern woman, just like the storybook porridge, is either too hot or too cold, but never just right.

In either case, the overarching message is that if women would just shut up, they would be tolerable again and then men would be liberated. But as Adams points out to his readers, that's an unlikely situation because women are too busy trying to shut men up to shut up themselves—and, there's little men can do about either situation (blog post from April 7th 2015). Adams reminds his readers that women have made much ado recently about male interruption of female speech. He even admits to being a (rather gleeful) culprit but ultimately accepts no blame, saying it's women's fault for saying useless or uninteresting things to begin with. But regardless of how much Scott Adams may or may not gain from being a serial interrupter, he admits that none of it really matters, because women have "won," their waves of feminism having washed away any competing male interests.

Adams goes on to argue that male humiliation is now so deeply institutionalized that men's persistent humiliation for simply being male is the default societal state (blog post from June 23rd 2016). Thus, the only realistic response any man can make is, in men's rights movement lingo, to "take the red pill", a reference from the movie *The Matrix* to a drug that makes its consumers see things as they really are.

Now, it may seem at this point that we're a bit far afield from gender stereotyping of women as shrews, but to paraphrase one feminist's assessment, Scott Adams is effectively saying that he thinks men just need to "man up" and accept their subjugation, because women won't understand their arguments and won't stop complaining even if they did.

Men Have It at Least as Bad

The Men's Rights Movement and men's rights activists attempt to borrow legitimacy from the very social movements many of them abhor by couching their views in terms like fairness, equivalence, nondiscrimination, equality, and justice. Both a central theme and primary complaint, men's rights movement groups like to gaslight the rest of us by claiming the state of affairs for typical men is a least as bad if not worse than that of women. On this point, Scott Adams heartily agrees: "STOP TELLING ME IN YOUR MIND THAT WOMEN HAVE IT WORSE IN THIS COUNTRY THAN MEN!" (blog post from June 23rd 2016).

But in fact Adams approaches this issue from a fairly different angle than men's rights activists. To begin with, he soft-pedals some of the more common men's rights movement rhetoric regarding significant inequalities between groups, saying that dealing with occasional maltreatment is a worthy cost of maintaining some semblance of a world in which, should the need arise, he can count on having a manly man pull him from a burning car (blog post from March 27th 2011). Thus, rather than focusing on issues like circumcision, conscription, false rape, or parental rights, Adams contends instead that men's psychological state of real or imagined humiliation and suffering is sufficient alone to define their experiences as worse than women's. For example, imminent death constantly hangs over their heads since, in Adams own words, "any solution to a problem that involves killing millions of adult men is automatically on the table" (blog post from November 17th 2015).

In a blissfully un-woke display of traditional American masculinity, Scott Adams has developed his own variation of the "Goldilocks Dilemma" in which he argues for the validity of men's rights movement issues and a recognition of men's significant suffering while simultaneously castigating men who talk about these issues and feel as though they are psychologically suffering, urging them to stop whining: "Now I would like to speak directly to my male readers who feel unjustly treated by the widespread suppression of men's rights: Get over it, you bunch of pussies." Naturally, a variety of female attitudes and actions have contributed to this massive pussification.

So What's the Point, You Angry and Hysterical Feminists?

At this point, we have probably angered more than a few *Dilbert* fans who are wondering if we read the comic and wondering why they should care about the waves of feminism. To these readers we respond that *feminism* is not a dirty word and that you are deluded and ignoring a virtual consensus in academia if you think we live in a matriarchy.

We see Scott Adams, in his blog posts, as an interesting combination of Dilbert, Dogbert, and Catbert and we, the authors of this chapter, are best represented as Alice and Tina. And probably the best way to deal with us is the same way you would deal with children and the mentally handicapped. Just saying.

10
Intelligence and Duh-mocracy

BEN SAUNDERS

In *The Dilbert Future*, Scott Adams distinguishes two kinds of people. First, there are the bright, attractive people who read *Dilbert* books (and, we like to think, this book). Then there are all the other idiots.

Scott calls these idiots "induhviduals." They're probably dumber than their smartphones. You likely know some. You may even work with them. If so, you'll doubtless know how frustrating they are to live with. They make things difficult for the rest of us.

Working with induhviduals is bad enough. But, in a democracy, these people also have a say over how the country's governed. They get a vote, the same as the rest of us! You may put a lot of thought into how to vote, reading party manifestos, following the news, and the like. But your vote can get canceled out by some idiot who votes for Candidate A rather than Candidate B, because he has nicer hair.

This seems like a bad way to run a business, so why do so many people think that this is the right way to run a country? Wouldn't it be better for everyone if only the smart people were in charge?

Diluting Intelligence

Scott points to a dilemma for democrats. If smart people are just as divided as everyone else, then intelligence is irrelevant to political decisions. That's rather disappointing. But if

113

smart people mostly agree, then democracy dilutes their influence. That's hardly welcome either.

Imagine one hundred people are choosing between two options, A and B. (Use whatever examples you like. Have B be something that seems like a good idea to induhviduals, but really isn't.) Suppose twenty of these people are smart. Sixteen of these smart ones favor option A, while the other four prefer option B. The other eighty are induhviduals, of whom thirty-two prefer option A and forty-eight favor option B. This means there's an overall majority of 52 to 48 in favor of option B.

	Option A	Option B
Smart people	16	4
Induhviduals	32	48
Total	48	52

Because most people are induhviduals, a fairly small majority (48 to 32, or 3:2) among them is enough to produce an overall majority for option B. This is so even though the smart people overwhelmingly favor option A. Personally, I'd rather go with the smart people here, but, when everyone votes, the induhviduals drown them out.

This example shows how intelligence can be diluted by democracy. The word 'democracy' comes from the ancient Greek *demokratia*, meaning rule by the people. But, if most people are induhviduals, perhaps it's better described as duh-mocracy or rule by idiots.

Many philosophers have criticized democracy along these lines. Plato attacked the ancient Athenian democracy of his day for neglecting wisdom and expertise. If you're sick, he asked, what would you do? Consult a physician with years of medical training or, instead, have everyone take a vote on the appropriate treatment?

It'd be ludicrous to let the unqualified masses make medical decisions but, Plato accused, this is what democratic rule amounts to. Ordinary people with no specialist expertise make decisions over all areas of life—including healthcare policy—paying no heed to those with relevant knowledge.

Plato's preferred alternative to democracy was rule by philosopher-kings. That's not so surprising, given that he was a philosopher himself, but his critique of rule by the ignorant masses is still forceful, even if we're suspicious of his proposed substitute.

Electoral Exclusions

Some contemporary philosophers agree with Plato. Jason Brennan from Georgetown University argues that many people are too ignorant or unreasonable to be given the vote. He doesn't call these people induhviduals—instead he labels bad voters either "hobbits" or "hooligans"—but they must be the people he has in mind.

Brennan proposes that the vote should be restricted to informed and reasonable people. He calls these people Vulcans to emphasize their rationality. Presumably, being smart people, they'd also be *Dilbert* fans. That's why the *Dilbert* fan club is called "Dogbert's New Ruling Class."

Brennan proposes disenfranchising induhviduals. Though he doesn't spell this out himself, this amounts to restricting the vote to members of Dogbert's New Ruling Class. Duhmocracy is replaced by what he calls an elite electoral system.

Excluding people from the vote is dangerous. Many groups, including women and blacks, were unjustly disenfranchised until relatively recently. But Brennan insists that his elite electoral system isn't like these past injustices. No one will be excluded on the basis of features like race or sex. Rather, there'd be a test to sort the smart people from the induhviduals. (Perhaps we could show people *Dilbert* strips and see who finds them funny. Those who do are obviously the smart ones.)

Requiring people to pass a test before being allowed to vote may seem unjust. But we require people to demonstrate their competence before they can do other things like drive or practice medicine. Why not test people before they vote, too? These are all activities that expose others to danger. This suggests that they should be regulated in the interests of public safety. Voter licences may prevent induhviduals from voting for bad ideas and wrecking things for the rest of us.

Of course, bad voters don't expose others to risk of *physical* harm like bad drivers do. Not all harm is physical, though. For instance, we can be harmed emotionally or financially. Bad decisions can cause many kinds of harm, as those who've been subject to random acts of management are aware. If politicians crash the economy, you could lose your job. While this might have its attractions, it's still a significant harm. (Unless you're rich enough that you don't need the job; in which case, why haven't you quit already?)

Another objection to voter licensing is that it threatens people's self-esteem. One problem with induhviduals is that they rarely realize their own stupidity. Being officially labelled an induhvidual may be demeaning.

Brennan points out that we already exclude some people, such as children, from voting. We don't generally worry that this is demeaning to those excluded. However, age thresholds exclude all children, without judging any particular child. It's not so nice for the smarter children that they have to wait for the rest of their peers to catch up, but at least no child need feel that they personally are judged to be incompetent. Everyone can tell themselves that they're one of the smart ones.

Failing a test is more demeaning than being excluded on grounds of age, because it singles out particular people as incompetent. It's precisely *because* the test is supposed to measure how smart you are that it's demeaning to fail it and be officially labelled an induhvidual. Failing tests doesn't feel good unless you're too oblivious to even notice. (One of my favorite *Dilbert* strips ends with Dilbert observing that his boss keeps failing the Turing Test!)

So, using a test to identify the induhviduals can be demeaning for those so identified. But that's not necessarily a decisive objection. We wouldn't let an unfit person drive a car or practice medicine simply to spare their feelings. Why should voting be different? Is it worth exposing the rest of us to harm to spare the feelings of induhviduals?

You might reply that the right to vote is unlike the right to drive because of its symbolic importance. Being granted the vote expresses that your interests and opinions matter. While we don't all agree about political matters, these decisions will affect the whole society. Granting everyone a vote recognizes that we share a common fate together. Being denied the vote suggests that you're somehow inconsequential. So everyone, even induhviduals, ought to have a vote.

Shares in Society

Once we rule out excluding induhviduals, it may look like we're committed to accepting duhmocracy. But there's another possibility. Instead of restricting the vote, we might reject the insistence on equality (one person, one vote). Maybe some people should have more votes than others, preventing their voices from being drowned out.

One possible reason for unequal voting would be to give those more affected by decisions more say. If the justification for including everyone is that we all have a stake in what happens to our community, perhaps those with a greater stake should have a greater say. This explains why those with more shares get a greater say over business decisions than those with fewer shares. Could we apply this principle to political decision-making?

A problem with this proposal is identifying who has a greater stake in the political community. Membership of political communities isn't usually something that comes in degrees. You're either a citizen of the society in question or you aren't. We may think that this is unlike the business world where we can distinguish between long-term employees and those on short-term or casual contracts, or interns like Asok, who aren't full members of the company.

However, there are groups of people who acquire membership and voting rights. Immigrants who eventually naturalize would be one example. Children are another. In both cases, there's no sharp dividing line between those who should be excluded and those who should be included as equals. Maybe there's some middle ground and perhaps it's sensible for people in this transitional phase to acquire voting rights gradually.

Partial inclusion would distinguish new members of the community from more established members. This might mean people having voting rights in only some elections (local ones but not national ones). Alternatively, it might consist in something like their having half-votes in their first elections.

This proposal looks to your past history to justify your claim to inclusion. But if the reason for including people is their shared future—the fact that decisions made now will impact them together—then the past is of little relevance. Instead, we should be concerned with future membership. So, we might want to exclude those who are about to leave the community, since they won't be part of this shared future.

On this basis, it could be that those with a longer future should have more say. Perhaps younger voters should have a greater say over decisions with long-term impacts, such as environmental policy. They'll have longer to live with the consequences, so they have more at stake. Older voters will on average be less affected, as most won't have to live with decisions for so long.

These examples illustrate the difficulty of determining who's more affected by particular decisions. It's even harder when it comes to an election, which will influence a number of decisions for the coming term. Perhaps it's fair enough to assume that all members of the community will be about equally affected by the election of a government.

Extra Votes for the Smart

An alternative justification for unequal voting is that the wiser or more intelligent should have greater influence over decisions. This gives smart people more votes than induhviduals, without entirely excluding the latter. This was proposed by the nineteenth-century English philosopher and social reformer, John Stuart Mill.

Mill advocated expansion of the franchise, including to women, yet he distinguished between giving everyone a vote and giving everyone an *equal* vote. Mill suggested that almost everyone should have *at least* one vote. But he added that those who had demonstrated intellectual and moral superiority should have extra votes, since their opinions ought to carry greater weight.

This plural voting scheme was intended to serve two purposes. First, Mill considered it appropriate to give more say to smarter people rather than holding all opinions to be equal. Suppose that Dilbert and his Pointy-Haired Boss disagree over some engineering problem. The Pointy-Haired Boss should defer to Dilbert's greater expertise. So, why shouldn't those who know less about politics be similarly deferential when it comes to political disagreements?

Second, giving extra votes to the smart ones would enable them to protect their interests from the more numerous induhviduals. Mill worried that extending the vote to manual workers might lead them to pursue class-based policies. The masses of induhviduals might even seek to enslave the smarter minority and have them perform complex tasks like tying shoelaces and programming VCRs.

Suppose society consists of two groups, a smaller group of smart people and a larger group of induhviduals. If each person has an equal vote, the induhviduals are bound to prevail because there are more of them. But we could give extra votes to the smart people until each group had equal votes. This would create a delicate balance of power. Neither group would be able to dominate the other. Mill's hope was that only ideas that appealed to at least some of both groups would get passed.

Thus, Mill hoped that plural voting would reconcile universal voting and intelligent decision-making. Giving the smarter people extra votes to balance all the induhviduals was supposed to prevent democracy from descending into duhmocracy.

Identifying Who's Smart

Giving extra votes to smarter people may be all very well in theory. Trying to put such a scheme into practice raises some fairly obvious difficulties, though. The first problem is identifying who's smart. Perhaps we could simply check people's bookcases for *Dilbert* books, but even this isn't fool-proof. If induhviduals somehow cottoned on to what was happening, they might buy *Dilbert* books too in order to seem smart.

We don't all agree on who's smart. Take Wally, for instance. You might think he's not very smart, since he doesn't seem to do very much except sit around in his cubicle drinking coffee. But, others might reply that he must be very smart indeed, and for much the same reason. Given the ingenuity that he puts into avoiding work, perhaps he's cleverer than he looks. (This isn't difficult.)

One of Mill's suggestions was that we look to people's occupation for evidence of their intellectual capacities. A supervisor might have more votes than a manual worker, and a professional—like a lawyer or surgeon—more still. Obviously, this is a bit naive. Dilbert is far smarter than his Pointy-Haired Boss. The Pointy-Haired Boss once spent twenty minutes talking to himself when Dilbert hooked his speed dial to his cell phone. In fact, he's just the kind of induhvidual we don't want in charge.

Thanks in part to Scott Adams, we know that incompetent induhviduals rise through the ranks of management. Therefore, managers should have *fewer* votes, not more. We could give extra votes to those who actually know what they're doing: people like Dilbert, Alice, Ted, and perhaps even Wally (though he probably wouldn't bother voting anyway). But tying voting rights to people's jobs is still imperfect. It might mean that those who are smart but under-employed—like Asok, the intern with an IQ of 240, or Dilbert's strangely wise bin collector—would lose out.

While Mill's plural voting idea hasn't attracted many followers, the contemporary philosopher Robin Harwood has defended something similar. Harwood proposed that extra votes could be tied to formal educational qualifications. Graduating from high school might be worth ten votes, while a bachelor's degree could be worth one hundred.

Harwood argues that this proposal is likely to lead to better quality public debate and better political decisions, while also giving people an added incentive to pursue education. It'd mean that Asok's degree from the Indian Institute of Technology could entitle him to extra votes (assuming he's eligible to vote in the first place).

Attaching votes to educational qualifications may be better than attaching them to jobs, but it's probably still a bad idea. Dilbert and his fellow engineers presumably possess technical qualifications. Doubtless they're well qualified to solve *engineering* problems. But, this doesn't mean they're any good at solving *political* problems.

Alice may be good at her job, but her anger management issues might lead to some bad decision making. Wally is lazy and self-centered. Even Dilbert is socially inept. None of these characters seem to have the non-educational qualifications, such as empathy, that we'd want from a ruling class.

This highlights one flaw in Harwood's proposal. Qualifications in engineering don't necessarily make someone any better at making political decisions. Someone could know a great deal about engineering (or many other fields) without knowing anything about politics. If we want to identify people who'll make good political judgements, then we can't rely on general educational qualifications.

Engineering vs. Humanities

One possibility is to distinguish between different areas of expertise. Looking at Dilbert and his colleagues, we may decide that an engineering degree doesn't guarantee that you're a good political decision-maker—perhaps even the reverse! However, other forms of education may foster the qualities we want in our political rulers.

Martha Nussbaum defends a traditional liberal-arts education, including history, literature, and philosophy. She argues that such humanistic disciplines develop our critical capacities and empathy for other perspectives—features that, she claims, are crucial for democratic citizenship.

Perhaps Dilbert wouldn't be as socially inept if he'd studied liberal arts instead of engineering. This wouldn't necessarily make him more attractive to the opposite sex, but Nussbaum argues that he'd be a better citizen for it. Citizens in a democracy must be capable of understanding other points of view and sufficiently critical to distinguish reliable and unreliable information (or "fake news").

Nussbaum doesn't actually propose giving extra votes to those with liberal-arts degrees, even though she thinks they're better voters. In fact, she'd probably reject this. But, if she's right that these people are better voters, then giving them more votes might lead to better decisions.

However, there's still a problem identifying the better voters. Though Nussbaum describes her educational ideal as humanistic, it isn't simply a matter of the subjects studied. What matters to her is the approach to education. Nussbaum advocates education driven by curiosity and experimentation rather than rote-learning of facts. And so, while a science degree could be taught through rote-learning, it need not be. Students might be encouraged to explore rival hypotheses for themselves. Similarly, history students might consider differing interpretations of evidence, or their degree could be based around memorizing dates.

Knowing *what* someone studied doesn't tell us *how* they studied it. Someone with a history degree might still be an induhvidual. Moreover, I guess it's possible to find an engineer with social skills. As a result, granting extra votes only to those with qualifications in certain subjects also looks like a bad idea.

The Demographic Objection

There's another, more fundamental, objection to linking political power and education. Other things being equal, let's assume that more educated people are likely to make better decisions. But the trouble is that other things generally aren't equal. The more educated are not a random cross-section of society, differing from others only by being smarter. Rather, education tends to go hand in hand with other qualities, which might detract from someone's competence as a decision maker.

Suppose we decide that engineers are smart people and give them extra votes. This means Dilbert, Wally, Alice, Ted, and the other engineers will each have multiple votes. Non-engineers will only have one vote each. This includes the Pointy-Haired Boss, Carol his secretary, and Tina the technical writer.

Those who get the extra votes are not simply more educated. They're also mainly men. It's not that *all* men get extra votes, of course. But still, this proposal would result in men having more votes than women. If we're making a decision that primarily affects women, then an educated man might be a worse decision maker than a less educated woman. It'd certainly be reasonable for someone to worry that the educated group aren't better decision makers here.

Note that the worry *isn't* that they are worse *because* they're educated. There's no anti-intellectualism here. It can still be accepted that education improves decision making. However, the educated people are also distinctive in *other* ways, which may make them worse at making particular decisions. This needn't be sex. For whatever reason (and there can be a multitude), the more educated members of a society may be mostly drawn from a particular race, religion, linguistic group, economic class, or some other group entirely.

In all these cases, we might think that the benefits of education are offset by privileging some particular social group. We don't even have to assume that this is actually the case.

Many people think that democratic institutions should be ones that we can all accept. The mere possibility that plural voting could produce worse outcomes means that people can reasonably object to it. And so, plural voting can't be justified to everyone.

The Democratic Workplace

I started with the thought that we wouldn't run a business democratically, so why think it's the best way to run a country? But, having considered possible alternatives to democracy, such as an elite electoral system or plural voting, it seems they're all flawed in practice.

We may like the *idea* of rule by smart people, but we can't agree on who's smart. While we could seek to resolve this disagreement by voting on it, that simply recreates the problem: we end up being ruled by those that induhviduals think are smart. Regardless, any attempt to set up rule by smart people only is likely to be disappointing, especially for those that get labelled non-smart. So, perhaps equal votes for everyone is best in practice, even if not in theory.

If we accept this rather pragmatic case for democracy, it might lead us to reverse my opening question. Maybe we should make workplaces more democratic, rather than making politics more like the workplace. Since the Pointy-Haired Bosses and CEOs aren't even the smart ones anyway, perhaps businesses would make better decisions if everyone had a democratic say in them. But, that's a topic for another time.

IV

Comic-Strip Camus

11
Dilbert's Absurd World

ALEXANDER CHRISTIAN

One of the entertaining aspects of Scott Adams's *Dilbert* is its constant depiction of the absurdity of modern corporate culture. In the clutches of an obscure self-serving bureaucracy, which neither rewards professional skills nor encourages corporate responsibility, Dilbert and his more or less competent colleagues are bystanders fluctuating between consternation and resignation in view of blatant mismanagement.

Examples of this absurdity abound: Wally, a cynical office bum devoid of any ethical principles, manages for years to maximize his personal gain while minimizing his workload to the point of blatant refusal to work. Asok, although highly intelligent and skilled, only gets assigned to minor engineering tasks—if not outright ignored—and is a common target of cultural stereotyping. Most of this is caused by the utterly incompetent micromanaging Pointy-Haired Boss, who, though blessed with a skilled team of engineers, is not able to recognize his staff's talents. Although it's easy for the reader to point at the absurdity of busy work and ridiculous decisions in comic strips with sharp punchlines, it's more difficult to give a precise philosophical analysis of what absurdity actually is—both in general terms as well as in terms of blatant corporate stupidity.

Dilbert and his colleagues seem to be confronted with absurdity similar to the kind described by philosopher and Nobel Prize–winning author Albert Camus. Some of the characters even seem to wholeheartedly embrace their absurdity. Think of Dilbert resigning himself to his company's approach to increasing productivity: changing the dress code to "Business Dorky" (a red polo shirt and a badge on a lanyard) rather than getting rid of the incompetent corporate executives. Sure, Dilbert could openly revolt against it, intending to *really change something,* but instead he embraces the absurdity and takes on the new hip corporate insignia—making snarky remarks from time to time. Yet in Adams's depiction of the absurdities of modern corporate culture there are departures from the existentialist reasoning about the absurd.

The Absurdity of Human Life

Among the existentialist philosophers interested in absurdity, like Jean-Paul Sartre and Søren Kierkegaard, Albert Camus is surely the one whose writing and thinking is most pervaded by the notion of absurdity. For Camus, absurdity results from an insurmountable conflict between the human desire for significance, meaning, and mental clarity on the one side, and a cold, unresponsive world on the other. Based on Camus's extensive writing on absurdity, comprising novels like *The Outsider*, his philosophical essay, *The Myth of Sisyphus*, and his *Letters to a German Friend*, the absurd to him is an immediate insight into a discrepancy between our own belief system, aspirations, course of life and current experience. It is a moment of existential crisis, which can only be answered with suicide, a leap of faith, or an acknowledgement of our own absurd condition.

The absurd has its roots in worldly suffering and misery. Since Camus is an atheist, worldly suffering and misery is utterly senseless to him. He doesn't think it occurs as part of the grand plan of a benevolent god. The absurdity this lack of meaning creates is on a different scale than small everyday absurdities—like the newest generation of Apple MacBook lacking proper USB ports, so you can't connect a printer, thereby defeating the purpose of a computer for professional or semi-professional applications.

Camus has a more fundamental, grand-scale problem in mind. Consider the hundreds of millions of people who go to work every single day, hating their job, helping to produce goods unnecessary to human flourishing and then using a good share of their income to consume those goods and compete in races to the newest Apple gadgets. Their everyday efforts just magnify the fruitless searches for meaning.

For Camus, the absurd is the insight into this fact, that the human impulse to search for meaning in a meaningless world is necessarily futile, yet not without hope. In order to avoid resignation and languor—this is an idea picked up from the philosophy of Friedrich Nietzsche—Camus advocates for an active response: Without any hope for a divine intervention by a benevolent creator who listens to your plea for meaning, the human condition in light of worldly suffering should be a permanent revolt. Although a permanent revolt against the absurd is not a genuine solution to the problem, it nonetheless offers the opportunity to cope with the inherent need for meaning in a meaningless world. The existentialist recognizes absurdity and seeks salvation neither in suicide nor in faith. The former would be self-denial, the latter an irrational leap of faith.

Instead, in light of the absurd, we aspire to just keep going. A symbol for this struggle is the mythological character of Sisyphus. In *The Myth of Sisyphus*, Camus depicts the felicity of the absurd human in his serene and self-sufficient resignation: Sisyphus rolls a heavy boulder up a mountain slope every day. The boulder never rests on top of the mountain, but rolls right down again, and so Sisyphus repeats his pointless task over and again. This is how he revolts against the meaninglessness. The revolt doesn't resolve the conflict between the need for meaning and a meaningless world. Rather, it is essentially a forlorn but nevertheless revolutionary endeavor—like buying a Samsung smartphone in order to escape the need for an Apple device. What Camus has in mind is a stance of snide resistance against reality.

Scott Adams: People Are Idiots!

Scott Adams has two distinct ways to express absurdities in his comic strips: One is to include bizarre and unworldly elements, like animals speaking a human language (Catbert or Dogbert, for instance) or mythical figures (most notably the Devil in person or troll-like accountants). Occasionally Adams also depicts simply irreal behavior, like random acts of magic or rampant acts of violence, like Alice looking for a harpoon to shoot her idiotic superior.

Such kind of *irreal absurdities*, are ways to highlight the depiction of *actual absurdities*, like nonsensical design decisions in technical products, fantastical business plans, or failed attempts to organize business workflow.

Universities grant MAs and PhDs in economics and business administration to confirm that managers are able to act in a competent and rational way. So, shouldn't the mere presence of supposedly competent professionals prevent the occurrence of absurdities? Adams has an intriguing explanation of why absurd situations in workplace situations exist at all. His theory is: people are idiots. Let this deep anthropological insight sink in for a while! For Adams, everyone is an idiot, including himself. The crucial point is that people are idiots about different things at different times.

Don't take offense at the term "idiot." It just means that humans have differing cognitive abilities. Some people are good with fixing jammed fax machines, some people can communicate well with crackbrained colleagues in superior positions, and some people are really good at making coffee. The problem is that people in business environments do not properly communicate their skills and are forced to do things outside the range of their competence. Think of a manager who does not understand that it is absurd to ask engineers to build a battery powered device, with an LED indicating that the battery is dead.

Lacking individual skills or knowledge, for instance technical skills and knowledge about the most basic functioning of LEDs, is a cause of requests for absurd technical features.

According to Adams, absurdities emerge from cognitive inabilities and a lack of organizational structures in modern corporate entities that properly distribute the incompetencies of employees—most notably residing in management—with cognitive skills of other people. So, the two important ingredients of absurdities are ignorance about certain things relevant for making rational management decisions and a lack of communication between employees on various steps of the corporate ladder.

Unlike in our personal lives where we tolerate and maybe even expect irrational behavior and strange convictions, in our work environment we fall prey to the ill-conceived myth that strategic business and internal management decisions are thoroughly guided by logic and rational thinking informed by unbiased work experience and well-established economic theories. According to Adams, this is not the case. We can find just as much absurdity in the workplace as in everyday life. The difference is that absurdity is more noticeable in business environments, since we have the expectation that people who are idiots most of the time—who lack crucial cognitive abilities—all of a sudden switch on the rationality mode in their brain when they enter the office.

Absurdities in Modern Corporate Culture

There are ample examples of absurdities in modern corporate culture depicted in *Dilbert* comic strips. Adams captures the whole spectrum: In the context of business communication, he points out that so called mission- or vision-statements for technology corporations routinely consists of Dadaist-seeming strings of nonsense buzzwords. Take this mission statement for instance, which surely was the end-result of a complex armada of engineers, people from marketing, and the management department:

> Perform world-class product development, financial analysis, and fleet services using empowered team dynamics in a Total Quality paradigm until we become the industry leader. (*The Dilbert Future*, p. 36)

As far as product development is concerned, Adams indicates that a lack of basic technical expertise on behalf of management staff can lead to contradictory or nonsensical technical requirements which remain uncorrected, since management neither understands technical limitations, nor defers to the technical expertise of engineers. By far the most common type of absurdity depicted by Adams falls in the category of mismanagement in personnel and everyday office work. In several cases, Dilbert, Alice, and Asok, while themselves competent, observe blatantly incompetent managers becoming appointed as leads to engineering or programming projects, although they are utterly incapable of comprehending the projects.

Most absurdities in the universe of *Dilbert* result from decision-makers' ignorance. Yet, sometimes not intellectual incompetence, but downright malicious intent is the cause of absurdity. This is particularly apparent when bizarre and other-worldly characters come into play, like Catbert, the evil director of human resources, who comes along as a sadistic megalomaniac particularly fond of developing evil policies. Such policies include the requirement to schedule sick time before being actually sick or to declare the time spent in the bathroom as vacation time.

The engineers in Dilbert's universe, like Dilbert, Wally, and Alice, almost always show resistance against absurd business decisions, albeit in different ways: Dilbert is most often in an epistemically privileged position, so that the reader can assume that Dilbert is totally aware of the idiotic tendencies of his colleagues or superiors, which lead to absurd decisions. Also, in a number of cases Dilbert seem to subtly revolt against something he deems absurd. For instance, when giving a presentation about the progress of a project, he casually expresses his disregard for his usually absentminded listeners:

> This next transparency is an incomprehensible jumble of complexity and undefined acronyms.

You might wonder why I'm going to show it to you since the only possible result is to lower your opinion of my communication skills.

Frankly, it's because I like making complex pictures more than I like you.

Wally, one of the oldest engineers in the company, has developed intricate arguments and mechanisms to avoid actual work. Among these mechanisms to avoid working for Pointy-Haired Boss are the Wally Reports he gives at staff meetings. These reports detail at considerable length his weekly accomplishments, which often consist in writing the report, or give a full account of trivialities or his emotional state during workday. Alice is depicted as an honest, hard-working engineer, who never receives credit for her solid achievements and is a constant object of sexist discriminations. Her resistance against absurdities resulting from errant management decisions frequently takes the form of physical violence against co-workers or management.

Absurd, All Too Absurd

Is the absurdity Dilbert experiences an existentialist kind of absurdity? We should note three key differences.

Pervasive absurdity vs. contained absurdity: When existentialists speak about absurdity, they mean a deeply troubling experience, a loss of purpose that pervades everything in your everyday experience of life. It results in a personal crisis, since the world is unresponsive to your wishes and desires for a meaningful life. That is why you can't leave a place, say your workplace, and leave existentialist absurdity behind. The same is not true for the type of absurdity that Adams illustrates. Here, absurdity is contained, say in an open-plan office or a cubicle. Contained absurdity can be left behind when you leave your workplace and go home after a few hours of mindless web-browsing, daydreaming or cigarette / coffee / [insert recreational drug of choice here] break. Office workers can to some extent escape contained absurdity, since it exists at a certain place and time. In contrast, existentialists can't escape this feeling.

Metaphysical vs. epistemic reasons for absurdity: The second important distinction concerns the causes of absurdity. For Camus, existentialist absurdity results from metaphysical features of the world, that is, fundamental facts about the way the world is. The world out there contains office buildings, cubicles, fax machines, but also buttercups and sandwich shops. Stock prices rise and fall, people launch companies and declare bankruptcy. Illustrious as it might seem, this world is unfortunately unresponsive, it severely limits our capacity to fully determine our fate. In some sense, we are all just helpless corporate drones waiting for retirement. We see that Adams's theory about the cause of contained absurdity in business is quite different from the existentialist perspective. For Adams, absurdity originates in humans, whose cognitive limitation crop out in particular during work days.

Recognition vs. bewildered amusement: Finally, and this is directly connected to the aforementioned distinction between metaphysical and epistemological reasons for absurdity, Camus and Adams propose different coping strategies for absurdity. Camus plays through three possible ways to deal with pervasive absurdity: committing suicide, turning to religion, or recognizing the absurdity of human life and revolting against things you yet can't change. Opting for the third alternative seems to be the most rational way for Camus, although there is no solution to the problem of pervasive absurdity. The original problem of contained absurdity depicted in Adams's comic strips, which are centered around dysfunctional business environments in tech-industry, is quite different. Things like ineffective employee recognition programs and meaningless business-speak in corporate mission and vision statements could in fact be changed. Absurdity in corporate culture is not a result of some kind of essential condition of our world. It is something that someone—probably someone from management, like Catbert or Pointy Haired Boss—did to the business culture, and in view of the resulting absurdity, we know the solutions. Give honest, proper credit for good work and formulate a precise, realizable business plan, so that everyone knows what to do. However, Adams's reaction to absurdity is very different: he recommends bewildered amusement. This is a different state of mind than existentialist recognition and revolt.

Beyond Bewildered Amusement

One attractive feature of existentialism is its liberating stance towards absurdity. While the concept of existentialist absurdity might convey an impression of helplessness and resignation, the opposite is true: For an existentialist like Sartre, individuals express their own will only in view of absurdity. Once asked whether Sartre felt oppressed in Paris occupied by Germany during the Second World War, he pointed out the liberating effect of the awful conditions. This gave him the opportunity to express his sense of morality both in friendships as well as in political and cultural activism. For Camus, the case is similar: when recognizing absurdity, we aren't forced to surrender. We rather find ourselves in a state of revolt against the absurd that we deem a hindrance to our wish for a meaningful and responsive world.

On a superficial level, Adams seems to be completely in line with Camus's conception of the absurd and surely some of the characters in Dilbert's universe seem to have adopted a stance of permanent revolt. But is this really the case for Scott Adams? In the *The Dilbert Principle*, he writes:

> It's useless to expect rational behavior from the people you work with, or anybody else for that matter. If you can come to peace with the fact that you're surrounded by idiots, you'll realize that resistance is futile, your tension will dissipate, and you can sit back and have a good laugh at the expense of others. (p. 11)

This might seem like something an existentialist in the tradition of Camus would say. But Adams's response is in fact cynical! He recommends acceptance, not as a first, but the ultimate step. It is recognition minus the revolt.

Adams carefully describes the reasons for absurdities in modern corporate culture and traces them back to the ignorance of those engineers, office workers and in particular managers, who are—for intellectual reasons—unable to discharge their professional tasks. Absurdity is neither pervasive nor a result of the metaphysical condition of human existence. It is rather a contained problem, which is open to a rational solution.

In every comic strip about mismanagement, bizarre technical decisions or errant coping mechanisms shown by corporate personnel, the reader immediately sees what's going wrong. And, curiously enough, the solution is often obvious. Maybe bewildered amusement is just a first step toward realistic expectations in a corporate culture where the occurrence of absurdities is at least reduced.[1]

---

[1] I would like to thank Frauke Albersmeier and Daniel Yim for their kind comments and corrections.

12
Dilbert Is an Asshole and That's Why He'll Never Be Happy and Nobody Loves Him

CHARLENE ELSBY AND ROB LUZECKY

Scott Adams's character Dilbert is an engineer who works in the middle of some kind of hellish bureaucracy, where every day he's confronted with the absurd and chooses to ignore it. We see his daily troubles, his foibles, his reflections, and his attempts to achieve for himself some bit of happiness, however small. He fails, and his relatable character flaws lead us to sympathize with him, his small problems and his small life. We get the sense of our own smallness in the grand scheme of things, completely absorbed in petty day-to-day concerns in which we can all find some bit of ourselves and our own lives.

Dilbert's existence, however, is a glorification of the worst parts of humanity, and it precludes him from ever being happy. *Eudaimonia*, usually translated as "happiness" but also as "flourishing," is an Aristotelian concept used to describe the ideal state of the human being, or the purpose of human existence to which all other purposes are subordinate. *Eudaimonia* is achieved by the individual who most fully exemplifies what it is to be human—what it is that we do that nothing else does, the thing that makes us human.

Eudaimonia is a state of the soul of the virtuous person, who has dedicated their life to exemplifying the best aspects of humanity—our capacity to reason about abstract concepts like being, truth, and the good. Dilbert's pedestrian existence leaves him fully ensconced in the relatively unimportant things, things that only seem important because the boss says they're important, or because your whole worldview is screwed up due to the pathological acceptance of some human conception of value that doesn't hold up in any other context than the one in which you presently live. (Remember your schooldays, when you could win a plastic trophy the teacher bought from the dollar store as a prize for some competition or other that has absolutely no applicability in the real world? Yeah, turns out nobody cares. Seemed pretty important at the time, though.)

Outside of the corporate mindset, "Employee of the month" means nothing. It's an arbitrary designation based on a concept of what constitutes a worthy employee, which is a messed up way of conceiving of humans only according to their capacity to produce profit for an entity run by other humans who determine their own self-worth based on how much money they can squeeze out of other people before they rebel.

According to Aristotle's *Nicomachean Ethics*, being a virtuous person is necessary if you're ever going to have a meaningful relationship with other humans. Essentially, *we only like good people*, and only good people are capable of appreciating other good people.

Dilbert's constant failure to achieve happiness occurs because he lives a miserable life, and because he's miserable, he'll never have a meaningful relationship. But it's not a matter of happenstance that Dilbert is so miserable. He chose that life. At literally any given moment, he could decide not to be a boring engineer whose work ethic leaves a lot to be desired, talking to a dog and a rat he named after himself, probably because he's so narcissistic that he can't even imagine something existing that has nothing to do with him.

Sometimes, he comes close to the edge of recognizing what an asshole he is, but then he always makes some excuse for why it's someone else's fault and continues living on, *intentionally* oblivious to the actual reason for his misery—which is him. He is a textbook example of what Sartre calls bad faith (*mauvaise foi*). He's not blissfully ignorant; he actually sees, every so often, the edge of the abyss which, should he choose to recognize it, would lead to an existential crisis that would eventually make him a better person. But instead, he runs away from the abyss, because at the most fundamental level of his existence, he thinks he's doing great. *He thinks he's doing fine and if he didn't, he would change.*

In general, we act the way we do because we think it's the best thing to do. And if we didn't think something was the best thing to do, *we wouldn't do it.* Dilbert's meaningless existence continues because, although he at any moment could choose to behave differently, to reflect on his misery and actually do something about it, he really thinks he's doing just fine. Dilbert's existence is a *willful*, *purposeful* exhibition of some form of reduced humanity, a cog in the wheel of an unreflective system, and he likes it that way. That's why he'll never be happy and nobody loves him.

Dilbert Is a Terrible Human

Every so often, usually because Dogbert points it out, Dilbert verges on the recognition of some universal truth that, should he choose to incorporate it into his worldview, would make him a better person. Instead, he willfully rejects that truth in favor of remaining comfortable, by continuing to do the same old thing despite the fact that all of the evidence so far should lead him to believe that he is *not* doing fine.

Like any asshole, he tries to re-prioritize his existence so that what he does well becomes the most important thing. *It's okay that he's bad with women, because he's a smart engineer*, he'll tell himself. *And one of these things is way more important than the other*. But it's not, and he's deluding himself. It's the women's fault, he claims. In the first few years of the Dilbert comic, we see him going on dates with a multitude of women, but only *one* date per woman. After that, we assume they run screaming into the woods, because they're not so deluded about Dilbert's insufficiency as a human being.

His complete unwillingness to examine his own existence and determine that maybe latent misogyny is not the way to relate to women is probably a factor. In any case, he'll be forever alone just because he's not a good person, and he's not even trying to be one. At the same time, he seems to think that he's entitled to the attention of women, and not just any women—attractive women, which he infers (on May 4th 1989) to exist "only in white Volkswagen rabbits and aerobics classes."

He has very high standards for such a mediocre puddle of human misery, and it's clearly not his fault that he's by some mystery of the universe unable to meet an attractive woman who's going to give him the loving he has earned simply for existing in the universe. In 1990–1991, Dilbert has a couple of dates that last more than one strip—with an obese woman, a witch and a literal dog (trapped in a woman's body), during which we can gain some valuable insight into why it is, perhaps, that his romantic adventures are always so brief. He thinks he deserves better, even though he's a terrible human being.

If Dilbert recognized his inadequacies, and we mean *really* recognized them, he would at least try to do something differently. But he doesn't. Instead, he makes jokes about his own insecurities. There's a whole series of strips from 1990 where Dilbert's ego becomes a character, only to be squashed by his own insecurities. He's actually claiming to be a very insecure person while, at the same time, believing that he deserves all of the good things in life without having to put in any effort whatever. *This is bad faith.*

Bad faith is a concept from existentialism that Jean-Paul Sartre uses to describe someone's state when they engage in life in an *insincere* or *inauthentic* fashion. Generally intimidated by the consequences of accepting some truth that they have come to recognize, they instead willfully reject that truth in favor of living a more comfortable lie. They tell themselves that they are living that lie for some legitimate, believable reason, but really they have recognized something unnerving with themselves or the universe and have *chosen* not to deal with it. That's one of the necessary features of a *bad faith* existence—that in order to be in bad faith, you have to first recognize what it is you're too afraid to live with. There's a difference between someone who fails at romantic relationships and can't conceive of the reasons why and someone who does conceive of the reasons why but *decides* to believe something else instead.

On April 20th 1990, Dilbert reflects to Dogbert, over the course of three panels:

> "About 400 women turned me down for dates this year. I can only conclude one thing . . ."
>
> Dogbert asks, "No quality women?"
>
> Dilbert responds, "Exactly."

On May 8th 1990, Dilbert notices that all of the "cool guys" use "gentle kidding" with women. Then he sees a woman on the street and says to her, "Excuse me, Miss, does your face hurt? It's killing me!" while *giggling and snorting*. And when the woman rams him into a trash can, he doesn't then infer that maybe that was a bad idea. Maybe women don't like it when you insult them and laugh at them. Maybe calling women ugly isn't actually a form of "gentle kidding", as he believes. Instead he rationalizes, "The cool guys must hate it when this happens to them."

These examples show that not only is Dilbert *not trying*, he's *trying not to*. He's *trying not to* recognize that he's a terrible human who treats people poorly and *maybe that's why* they don't like him.

Speaking of not trying, he doesn't even put effort into his work, even though it seems to be the only thing giving meaning to his pitiful life. He has the standard concerns of any entitled white dude—the feeling of not getting enough recognition from his superiors while at the same time joking about how little effort his job requires. It's not that he has no idea that he's performing to subpar standards. He knows he is, he jokes about it, and he still thinks he deserves better.

At one point, he even has the audacity to tell his boss about how stupid bosses are in general, and he suggests switching places with his boss to increase productivity. What kind of arrogant fuck thinks he can get away with that bullshit? And the rest of the time, when people ask him about his work, he makes up words and tries to overcomplicate things to sound smart, just so that people will get confused and leave him alone. He shows no respect for the intelligence of his colleagues and overtly rejects their attempts to show interest in his activities, instead making them feel stupid in order to cover up the fact that he doesn't do his job. *What an asshole.* He's an asshole who *tries* to make people feel stupid when they try to talk to him, and then *he complains that he's lonely.* Just *wow.*

And He'll Never Be Happy

Happiness is a state of the soul of the virtuous person. The prefix "eu" means "good" or "well," while "daimon" is the Greek word for "spirit" (or "demon"). To be happy is to literally have a *good* spirit. To *get* happy, you have to be virtuous, and to be virtuous, you have to do good things, and in order to do good things, you have to first know what is good. And Dilbert doesn't.

Given the insurmountable evidence for the idea that Dilbert is indeed living the life he *chose*, we have to wonder how it is that he justifies it to himself. We believe that he finds his flaws endearing, and that while he claims to be insecure, he is actually quite comfortable with his character flaws, to the point where he has managed to reconceive of them as *good*.

Flaws are not good. That's why they're called flaws. To think that they are good is a basic contradiction in terms, yet one that Dilbert *must* believe, given that he seems to think himself entitled to a fulfilling career and the admiration of others. He no longer has any concept of what is good, and therefore no motivation to *do* what is good. He is therefore precluded from developing the character virtues that, Aristotle says, are necessary to call a person happy.

Whether someone is happy is a judgment we can make about a person at the end of their lives, based on all that they have been and done. As Aristotle says in Book I of the *Nico-*

machean Ethics, "For one swallow does not make a summer, nor does one day; and so too one day, or a short time, does not make a man blessed and happy."

Besides insulting his boss and treating women like objects who owe him something, Dilbert doesn't do much of anything. Instead, he *persists*, not like someone making a valiant effort to complete a difficult task, but more like a mold that, no matter how many times you bleach it, continues to grow behind the refrigerator, just always there. No matter how much social conditioning he is exposed to through other people's reactions to his blatant failures as a human being, he persists in his effort to *continue. As is.*

For Aristotle, character virtues are all "means." They're an equilibrium between two vices, where the vices and the virtue are part of the same spectrum. Too little of something is a vice, too much of something is a vice, but just the right amount is a virtue. Where courage is a virtue, cowardice is a vice—courage is the state of having just the right amount of fear, while the coward is *too* afraid. A virtuous person has a good amount of ambition or pride, while a vicious person is *too* ambitious or *un*ambitious. While a virtuous person might feel righteous indignation in the face of some injustice, the deficient person is spiteful, petty, mean, and feigns modesty.

A person who exemplifies all of the virtues will be courageous, temperate, liberal, magnificent, magnanimous, properly proud, patient, honest, witty, friendly, modest, and will respond appropriately in all sorts of circumstances. Dilbert is none of these things. Relative to all of the virtues that Aristotle claims are necessary to achieving a good state of the soul—that is to say, happiness—Dilbert is profoundly deficient. And he'll always be that way because he avoids all of the good things that lead to happiness, not out of some grand rebellion against the universe, but because he's pathetic.

In order to do what's good, you must know what's good, and that knowledge is achieved through reason. For Aristotle, there are types of reason, one of which we use to determine *what is good*, and another of which is a reason we use to determine *how best to achieve that good.* By constantly aiming at the good, humans are really aiming at happiness—the highest good for humanity. For no one asks seriously, "Why do you want to be happy?" and it is therefore the good to which all other goods aim. Why would you want to make money? To be happy. Why would you want a dog to talk to and walk around with? To be happy. And so on. But if you can't use reason properly to determine what the intermediate goods are on the way to happiness, then you won't be happy.

On December 13th 1989, Dilbert remarks to Dogbert, "Some say it is man's ability to reason which separates him from mere animals." That's true. Some do say that—people like Aristotle, who thought that our capacity to reason is what differentiates us from all of the other animals. When we aim at the highest good for humanity, we aim to express what it means to be human—and that is a "rational animal." Thus it seems that the way to happiness is to exercise reason, and that's just what Aristotle would say.

Dilbert, on the other hand, avoids the conclusion that he should be reasonable, by willful distraction. In response to Dilbert's observation, Dogbert responds, "Surely you realize that in the animal kingdom there is no equivalent to 'all-star wrestling'." And Dilbert laments, "Ooh—we're missing it right now." This is another overt foray into the land of bad faith, where Dilbert recognizes that the essence of humanity is to be rational, and *decides* to watch wrestling instead. The implied reasoning is that all-star wrestling is of a similar worth to reason itself, since it is similarly exclusive to humans, but just because only humans are capable of something or other, *that does not mean it is good*. There are many things that only humans can do that are either detrimental or just useless in regards to human happiness, and Dilbert is intentionally accepting bad logic in order so that he might go watch wrestling instead of bettering himself. He chooses to be unhappy.

Seriously

Simone de Beauvoir's concept of the serious man (from her book, *The Ethics of Ambiguity*) should really drive home just how it is that Dilbert has *chosen* to live miserably, and how he's not only responsible for his misery (in a causal sense), but how his pitiful mode of existence is actually a *moral failing*.

In the greatest book on ethics written in the twentieth century, the French philosopher Simone de Beauvoir specifies what sorts of people deserve to be punched in the face. Dilbert is definitely punchable. Writing right after the Second World War, Beauvoir knew that some of the worst people in the world are Nazis. (Sadly, this is a fundamental ethical truth that too many Americans have seem to have forgotten.) Of all the types of people that are deserving of a punch in the face, perhaps the most punchable, are what Beauvoir classifies as "serious men", who—more than anything else—value advancing up the hierarchy of the corporate or governmental system that they know is complete bullshit.

Beauvoir illustrates the nature of the serious man through the example of the colonial administrator who would gladly condemn a bunch of laborers to death, in order to complete the construction of a highway. What sort of monster thinks that his completion of a project is more important than the lives of workers? A serious man, that's who. It might be tempting to think of serious men as buffoons of diminished intelligence (not unlike a baboon flinging his own feces), but this is wrong. Beauvoir points out that serious men are intelligent enough to recognize that the system in which they operate is without moral justification *and* they also recognize the criteria that they must satisfy to achieve success in this system. Serious men are sell-outs, who know damn well that they have sold out and who are too morally vacant to give a shit. It's not just that the serious man's moral values are utterly skewed, it's that the serious man has decided that some artificial (corporate or governmental) system of values is more important than any moral system which values human life. The serious man is not deplorable. He is contemptible.

Dilbert is a serious man. In a series of comic strips that ran from December 16th 2017 to December 20th 2017 Dilbert points out that the corporation he works for has invented an "app" that is addictive. While he first seems to have some misgivings about the effects of the app, he quickly gets over any moral qualms when he is offered a raise to suppress his findings. Later on, Dilbert points out that the app has triggered a "Zombie Apocalypse." Even Dilbert's idiotic manager is alarmed by the threat of a bunch of desperate, emotionally isolated, half-mad people wandering around the streets looking for a dopamine fix. Dilbert assures him that this aspect of the app has been monetized. Further testing shows that the app causes a monkey to eat its own hand. Dilbert proudly reports these findings to a board meeting. He's the engineer who is responsible for the unleashing the technological equivalent of a biblical plague.

Dilbert has a funny haircut. He seems to be a mild-mannered office stooge who is just trying to get by. Dilbert might seem eminently insignificant, utterly ignorable, but he is, in fact, much worse. Dilbert is a serious asshole.

13
The Essence of Dogbert

ELLIOT KNUTHS

Dogbert, Catbert, Ratbert, and Bob the Dinosaur play a unique role in Scott Adams's *Dilbert* universe. On one hand, they are animals, and on the other, they're basically just human characters in animal bodies.

Sometimes they don't even behave like members of their own species. In a strip from May 16th 1989, Dogbert expresses a desire to become friends with other dogs but confesses he doesn't really know what ordinary dogs are like. Later, on August 18th of that year, Dogbert is taken aback when he encounters a normal dog. Despite, however, his resemblance and preference for humans, Dogbert is obviously still a dog. And this raises some interesting philosophical questions and challenges.

Is Dogbert a dog in the same way that your Labradoodle is? If so, is Dogbert *real* in some sense? Furthermore, how do our answers to these questions matter at all? Do they impact our appreciation of the *Dilbert* series or other works of fiction?

What Makes Dogbert Whatever He Is?

Metaphysics, classically but vaguely defined as the study of being, deals not only with what is but also with what could and could not possibly be. Put another way, it's the area of philosophy concerned with the nature of reality as it exists, apart from human experience.

147

One issue frequently discussed in metaphysics is which properties are essential to an object and which are those it has accidentally. Which properties must an object necessarily continue to possess in order to remain that very same object (its essential properties), and which could it lose without becoming something else (its accidental ones)? If essential properties change, then an object becomes something else. Accidental properties, on the other hand, may come and go without changing an object's identity. Plenty of philosophers reject the theory of essentialism just characterized, but this chapter will take it for granted, since it's a popular starting point for learning a little metaphysics.

For a concrete illustration of the distinction between essential and accidental properties, think about yourself for a moment. According to one popular type of essentialism, species essentialism, being human is one of your essential properties. You cannot both exist and fail to be human. You couldn't be a peregrine falcon or a pile of snow or the number seventeen or Bob the Dinosaur; you can only be a human person. Having hair, however, is an accidental property of yours (if you have it at all). You could lose all of your hair overnight or shave it all off in the morning and you would still be the same person you are right now.

Similarly, we can think about the essential and accidental properties of the characters in *Dilbert*. For example, Dogbert is essentially a dog. If you're reading a *Dilbert* strip and a non-dog character appears in it, you can, according to the species essentialist, be sure it is not Dogbert (assuming, of course, the non-dog is not really just Dogbert in disguise). The only plausible exception to this rule is that Dogbert might miraculously transform into some other object like a tree or a brick wall, which has happened in previous strips, for instance the one from October 31th 2003.

Transformations like these are incompatible with species essentialism, but for argument's sake, we'll proceed by assuming that Dogbert is essentially a dog. He's probably not essentially white, though. Imagine that, in a plot to win favor with Bob and Dawn, Dogbert drinks a potion that turns him green.

Although he now has a dramatically different appearance, he's still the same being he was before the potion. So, having white fur is an accidental property of Dogbert's, albeit one that, to my knowledge, remains present throughout the series.

The Modal Account of Essences

The distinction between essential and accidental properties discussed above has been around for millennia. Aristotle (384–322 B.C.E.) gave the first systematic account in his *Metaphysics*, written nearly 2,400 years ago. The idea of essences has remained important in Western metaphysics ever since. Despite its age, however, essence is not an unchanging or dusty topic in philosophy. In fact, a revolutionary new approach to thinking about essences emerged in the last century alongside developments in modal logic.

Modal logic is a special logical framework that helps philosophers deal with questions of *necessity* and *possibility*. When we talk about something being necessary, we mean it must be or must have been the way it is or was. When we talk about something being possible, we mean that it could have been different or it might be different in some way.

Modal logic is a powerful tool when thinking about what must be the case as opposed to what might have been the case or what could never have been the case. Although philosophers usually apply modal logic by using tons of abstract, quasi-mathematical symbols, they also employ it in less formal terms when appealing to *possible worlds*.

Philosophers say that necessary truths, such as facts from arithmetic like "2 + 2 = 4," are by definition true and can never be false. Thus, they are true in all possible worlds. Necessarily false statements which lead to contradictions, like "1 + 1 = 3," are not true in any possible world.

There is also much that lies in between the two extremes of necessary truth and necessary falsehood which might be true in some worlds and false in others. A proposition which might be true or false is a *contingent* one, depending on which world we consider. There are possible worlds where I have an uncle who is an avid *Dilbert* reader, but there are also possible worlds where I exist but do not have an uncle who reads *Dilbert*.

Keep in mind that references to possible worlds do not commit philosophers to believing in some comic-book-style multiverse where all possible worlds spatiotemporally exist in the same way our world does. Although some philosophers, like David Lewis (1941–2001), do endorse a position somewhat like this, many, probably most, philosophers view possible worlds as descriptions of ways the world could have been, not as other universes parallel to our own.

Modal logic works well with the concepts of essential and accidental properties. Those properties that an object or person possesses in all possible worlds (that is, possesses necessarily) are essential to that object or person. Those properties that an object or person does not possess necessarily, but still possesses in some possible world, are its accidental ones. So, looking back to our earlier examples, you are human in all possible worlds in which you exist, but you lack hair on your head in some, but not all, possible worlds in which you exist. Applying the same reasoning to Dogbert, because he is essentially a dog, he is a dog in all possible worlds where he exists. Likewise, there are one or more possible worlds where Dogbert has green fur at some point in time, and one or more possible worlds where he does not.

A popular approach among philosophers working in metaphysics is to treat possible worlds as abstract objects. Philosophers who believe in abstract objects consider them to be entities not located anywhere in space or time, but which nonetheless are as real as you or me. Typical examples of abstract objects include numbers, shapes considered in the abstract (*a* triangle, not *the* triangle you see in front of you), properties (like "being a dog"), and propositions. When thinking about possible worlds as abstract objects, you can think about them as sets of propositions, each of which exhaustively describes a way a world possibly could be. Relationships among properties can then be assessed in terms of when they hold and in which possible worlds they hold.

Consider the following properties: "being more than five feet tall," "being more than six feet tall," "having only brown hair," and "not having only brown hair." For all objects in all possible worlds, the property "being more than six feet tall" holds only if "being more than five feet tall" also holds, since nothing can be over six feet tall unless it's also more than five feet tall. But, an object can have the property of "being more than five feet tall" without having the property of "being more than six feet tall." There are also possible objects that exist that have the properties of "being more than five feet tall" and "having only brown hair." Likewise, "being more than five feet tall" is compatible with "not having only brown hair." No possible object has both the properties of "having only brown hair" and "not having only brown hair," simultaneously, as that would imply an impossibility.

Dogbert: King of Elbonia, Threat to Metaphysics

As mentioned earlier, we're assuming that Dogbert is essentially a dog. In the modal lingo of possible worlds, this means that Dogbert is a dog in all possible worlds where he exists. Suppose we also recognize that Dogbert is intelligent, speaks fluent English, and has worked as a CEO and a business consultant, because there is a possible world, the one described in *Dilbert,* where this occurs. From these observations and Dogbert's essentially being a dog, it follows that it is possible for a dog to be intelligent, speak fluent English, and work as a CEO or a business consultant.

The problem is this: suppose we're having a conversation about some company. I am considering buying stock in the company and you tell me that I ought to wait and see how the company's new CEO adapts before I decide whether to invest. I had not heard about the change of leadership that you had, so I know nothing about this new CEO. However, having recently read *Dilbert,* the idea of a canine CEO is fresh in my mind. I ask you whether the CEO is a dog or not. You likely chuckle at the absurdity of my question, or else politely ignore it, quietly suspecting I have gone mad. I persist, though, explaining that Dogbert was appointed CEO of Dilbert's company in the November 15th 2014 strip. Since being a dog is one of Dogbert's essential properties, the fact that Dogbert became a CEO means that there is a possible world where a dog is a CEO, so it's possible for dogs to be CEOs and my question is justified.

Is this too literal a reading of *Dilbert,* though? That's the worry. An approach like this allows facts internal to the *Dilbert* universe to influence our intuitions about what's true and false in the actual world. At the same time, we definitely *do* want to say that Dogbert has some of his properties essentially. The reason for this is that we want to be able to say that the assertions "Dogbert is essentially a dog" and "Dogbert is essentially a cat" are different because one is true and the other false. If we say that the first assertion is also false, then we cannot say anything at all meaningful about Dilbert's fictional universe. Thus, our explanation of exactly what the world of *Dilbert* metaphysically *is* must not logically undermine our self-evident ability to speak meaningfully about the world of *Dilbert.*

Furthermore, we don't want to prevent ourselves from saying that the scenarios presented in *Dilbert* have nothing to say about the real world. They would hardly be funny or worth reading if that were the case. A large part of the success of the *Dilbert* franchise comes from the way it mirrors American professional life. Scott Adams has even released *Dilbert*-themed books about professional life. Both *The Dilbert Principle* and *Dogbert's Top Secret Management Handbook* were bestsellers, which is pretty compelling evidence that *Dilbert* does reveal some insight about real life.

Three Ways to Solve It

The philosophical problem posed by Dogbert is now in sight. How might we resolve it? There are several popular ways of understanding fictions like Scott Adams's *Dilbert* universe that respond to the issues I've mentioned. They are *possibilism, Meinongianism,* and *creationism.*

Somebody who thinks authors do not *create* a fictional world but rather *discover* some non-actual possible world is a possibilist. Such a person might claim *Dilbert* actually does tell us something important about the metaphysical properties of dogs and CEOs. Philosophers who approach fictions this way believe that if the world of *Dilbert* described by Scott Adams could possibly exist, then the beings in it, like Dogbert or Bob the Dinosaur, can be discussed as though they exist in the actual world because they exist as abstract objects contained in a possible world (itself an abstract object).

Philosophers who view fictional beings as existing in a possible world are generally prepared to countenance the often-bizarre implications of fiction. In this case, someone who deems the world described in *Dilbert* a possible world will be committed to the possibility of a dog working his way up to a CEO position in a major company. On the other hand, this position arguably does the best job of explaining what we're doing when we discuss *Dilbert* and preserving our intuition that we can discuss the events which occur in *Dilbert* the same way we discuss events which happen in the actual world.

Meinongianism is a similar view, originally defended by the Austrian philosopher Alexius Meinong (1853–1920), which holds that all things that can be referred to have being in some sense, even if they are impossible objects which could never exist, like square circles. Impossible or fictional objects like square circles or Dogbert may not actually exist, but they do possess properties attributed to them (in the case of the square circle, the properties of being square and of being circular; in the case of Dogbert, the property of being a dog, being Dilbert's closest friend, and being a CEO). Meinongianism allows us to preserve the ability to speak meaningfully about Dogbert and his properties but at a high cost: we must also grant being to everything else we could speak of, including such impossibilities as square circles.

In the context of fictional objects, creationism is the view that fictions like Dogbert, Elbonia, and Dilbert himself are not discovered but made. Creationists would say that Dogbert is an abstract object, but one which, unlike eternal numbers and shapes, has a temporal beginning, namely at the moment when Scott Adams first imagined him. Thus, Dogbert's existence depends upon Scott Adams's existing and thinking up Dogbert.

According to the creationist, even though we can speak meaningfully about Dogbert in this world, there are worlds where we could not because Dogbert does not exist in those worlds. Such worlds include those where Scott Adams never existed or ones where, for one reason or another, he did not create *Dilbert*. This theory agrees with our intuition that Adams created, rather than discovered, Dogbert. It has its own weaknesses, though.

Imagine that, at the very moment that Scott Adams was creating *Dilbert*, another fellow, call him "Not-Adams" was independently creating the exact same fictional universe. The internal narratives and the characters are all identical. Now suppose that Scott Adams never existed, or for some reason never created *Dilbert*. If we grant that Not-Adams could create the same fictional universe at the same time as Scott, there should be no reason he could not likewise create it without Scott. If we believe that two different authors could possibly have created the same exact work of fiction, the view that fictional objects depend upon their creators for existence doesn't look too promising.

Fiction Shapes Reality

I have not attempted to argue that one of these three competing approaches to fictional characters is better than its alternatives, because each one has significant strengths and weaknesses. One thing we can surmise from the example of *Dilbert* is that even extravagant fictional worlds can parallel reality in insightful ways.

14
Of Course It Sucks— It's Work

ANDY WIBLE

No contemporary writer has brought out the doldrums of work better than Scott Adams, and no character expresses the plight of a disenfranchised employee better than Wally. When Wally is asked why he doesn't work much, he responds, "I figure there will be plenty of time to work when I am dead. The co-worker says back, "But you won't be here to do it." Wally says, "I guess you don't know what a perfect system looks like."

Old-Fashioned Hard Work

Why does Scott Adams have such a negative view of work? One answer is simply that it is work. Work is a necessary evil that we would avoid if we could. Lottery winners are most excited because they get to say those two words: "I quit." Work is labor, which is taxing, dull, and difficult. Work sucks. It is freedom-sapping and it stunts our growth as human beings. It is a daily humiliation, as Studs Terkel points out.

Scott Adams writes in *The Joy of Work,* "The only reason your company pays you is because you'd rather be doing something else. We work as long as we need to sustain ourselves and those who depend upon us, and then if we are lucky enough we can retire and enjoy what is really important in the world."

155

The classical Greeks, such as Plato and Aristotle, held this view of work. We are free, intelligent beings and work constrains us. Yes, we need to work, but we should work as little as possible. At the time slaves did much of the hard labor. Wealthy Greeks and Romans didn't arrange their lives around work. In fact, Aristotle taught students, but mostly he valued his leisure. His views caught on. In Rome, by the fourth century there were over 175 public festival days per year. The cultured and civilized avoided work because it numbed the mind.

In the past, the dehumanizing view of work focused on blue-collar work and hard labor. Work is bad, according to this view, because it's either backbreaking or else boring assembly-line work. This kind of work, goes the view, is monotonous and valueless. It has no intrinsic value and, consequently, neither do the people who do it. Robots could do it, and increasingly they do. Even educated engineers like Dilbert and his colleagues are constantly concerned that robots will take over their work.

Karl Marx's critique of capitalism makes this point. In a capitalist society, only products and profits matter. Workers become objects rather than subjects. Workers are dissociated from their work. Creativity is lost. Workers might as well be machines. Adams makes this point clear with his most disenfranchised worker Wally. Wally says to Dilbert, "You claim to be an introvert and yet, you never seem drained when talking to me." Dilbert responds, "That's because you don't put off a human vibe. I experience you the same way I do birds, furniture, and robots." "You totally get me," agrees Wally, to which Dilbert says, "Don't talk." Algorithms and robots are threatening to take over the engineering work that Dilbert and co-workers do, because they're already treated and treat each other as objects.

Even though workers hate their jobs, they need them and want them. A job allows us to buy the things that will make us fulfilled and happy. People are "working for the weekend" as is often said. The happiness which we get from houses, cars, beer, and family all cost money. Work, according to this view, has no value in and of itself. Work only has instrumental value. It is a tool to get what is really important, such as family, happiness, beauty, music, knowledge, and love.

What does this mean about a good work ethic? Should we work hard if work itself has no intrinsic value? Hard work has often been praised, especially in the United States. The Protestant work ethic remains an ideal, one that is believed to be necessary for achieving success in life. Americans work longer hours than citizens of most other industrialized nations in the world. The forty-hour work week is often thought to be a minimum which we should exceed. According to a 2015 Gallup Poll, Americans work on average 47 hours per week compared to around 35 hours per week in Norway, Italy, Denmark, and other European countries. Almost 40 percent of Americans working full-time said they worked more than fifty hours a week and they mostly had white-collar jobs. The harder we work and the more work goals we achieve, the more successful we are as persons. True American idols are people like Warren Buffett, a billionaire who works long hours well into his eighties.

Perhaps the best criticism of the hard work ethic comes from Wally. Why are we praising something inherently bad? Wally says, "Remember, Asok, success requires hard work and sacrifice." Asok replies, "Got it! I will work hard and sacrifice." Wally retorts, "I was going to say that is why you should avoid success. Who brainwashed you?"

Real success is found outside work and Wally is keen enough to realize that. We shouldn't want to be Warren Buffett because he needlessly works all the time. Americans go to work so much that they don't get to enjoy its spoils. We have all heard tragic stories of people who work long hours, ignoring their family, and who then die on the job. The Japanese language even has a word for it. "Karoshi" is death from overwork. Unfortunately, karoshi is alive and well. In 2017, a thirty-one-year-old Japanese reporter died of heart failure after working 159 hours of overtime in a single month. Perceived "success" killed her.

Another critique of the ethic of working hard is that it is a lie perpetrated by people in power. Adams's CEO yells to employees, "We can only succeed if we work harder than our competitors." Then he looks down at his phone that goes off, "oops, I gotta go. My helicopter is here to take me to my massage on my super-yacht." He looks up adding, "Stop staring at me. I only have to work harder than the other CEOs." As in Greece and Rome, the elite today know the importance of leisure over hard work. Without slaves that can be forced to do hard labor, lower-level employees are brainwashed into doing it for low pay. Tina realizes this when Pointy-Haired Boss says, "Remember, it is only work if you would rather be doing something else." Tina says, "I would rather be doing *anything* else." Pointy-Haired Boss replies, "Oh, in that case, you are trapped in a nightmare that never ends." Tina then muses, "I have a lot riding on the afterlife."

Tina's problem, namely that hard work fails to pay off in this life, was anticipated in the Greek story of Sisyphus. Due to his own self-aggrandizement, craftiness, and deceit, Sisyphus was condemned by the gods to roll a rock up a hill every day for all eternity, only to have it roll back down again every time. This is an analogy to our life. We get up, go to work, come home, eat, sleep, and then do it all over again the next day. Our lives seem as meaningless as that of Sisyphus. Dilbert says, "You know my life is an endless string of useless tasks orchestrated by idiots." The only hope seems to be getting the rock to the top of the hill, as Tina might imagine happening in a meaningful afterlife. This pipe-dream is one that Tina seems to disbelieve even as she entertains it.

Yet an important difference between Sisyphus's situation and ours is that we have life outside of work. We can find happiness and meaning outside work with family, friends, quiet contemplation, and hobbies, after rolling the rock. Dates aside, even Dilbert seems to enjoy some of his time outside of work with his friends Dogbert and Ratbert. Thus, if work has no inherent value, people must do more than work if they are to live a meaningful life. The key is to always focus on what's really important, such as happiness and friendship with others. People in countries such as Denmark and France are doing a better job than those in the United States, for they rank higher on the happiness index, partly because they work fewer hours and vacation more.

There are a couple of criticisms of this classical view of work, which Adams seems to support with his humor. First, we can't separate our jobs from the rest of our lives. We are our work. Our work affects us when we work and when we don't work. There is overflow. Anyone who has worked has also lost sleep over what happened at work. Also, our identity is connected closely to our work. When meeting someone new for the first time we generally ask, "So, what do you do?" Read any obituary to see the importance of work to a person's identity. We are our jobs, and if we are not fulfilled at work, we won't be at home. As Al Gini says in his book, *My Job, My Self*, "I work, therefore I am." Dilbert does not have a meaningful life at home for many reasons, but work is not helping. Dilbert thinks, "It's another useless day at work with no accomplishments. Luckily I have a meaningful life at home." When he gets home Dogbert says, "Ratbert broke the Xbox." Dilbert replies, "GAAA! I have nothing."

Finally, we spend a third or more of our adult lives working. Shouldn't that third of our life be fulfilling? Sure, we need to do some things we don't want to do in life, but a better life is one where the work that we do is enjoyable. Our work brings us meaning as well as our home life. Some even believe work is necessary for a person to live a meaningful life.

Fulfilled Workers

Gini supports what philosopher Joseph Desjardins appropriately calls the "human fulfillment" model of work. This view holds that work is a necessary activity, through which people develop into their full potential as human beings. Work doesn't thwart meaning; work is required for people to have meaning in their lives. Life without work is not worth living. Areas with high unemployment tend to have high rates of depression and other mental health problems, even when their basic needs are being met. It's not just money they are lacking, it is work.

The human fulfillment view accepts the Greek view that all humans have the potential to live fulfilling lives. It differs by claiming that work, and not just leisure, can provide fulfillment all by itself. Warren Buffett has a successful life because he is fulfilled through his hard work. It isn't a job that he has to do; it's calling that he loves to do. Even his book is called *Tap Dancing to Work*. He's not doing it for the money. He plans to give most all his money away to charity after he dies. Adams satirically points out this need for treating people better in work. People can relate to what he says. No one wants to be treated or to treat people the way that Pointy Headed Boss does.

Good work helps to bring meaning to our lives by providing us with virtues. Work organizes our lives. Economist E. F. Schumacher says that good work brings creativity, challenge, development, honesty, and an element of Beauty, Truth, and Goodness. Every employer should strive help develop these qualities. Adams, in his book *The Joy of Work,* discusses the importance of creativity in the workplace and allowing time for creativity. He says we should manage creativity and not time. Some people manage time and are always filling any hole in their schedule. Adams believes that good work allows for strategic times where you are not technically busy and can be creative. Donald Trump now calls this "executive time." Creativity is something that makes jobs meaningful. As the robot once said to Dilbert, "Someday robots will do all of the technology work and humans will only do creative jobs."

You might object that it's impossible for every job to allow for creativity. A blue-collar worker doesn't have two hours of executive time in the morning to be creative. But while the amount of creativity may be relative to the job, all jobs should allow for some. For example, many blue-collar jobs incentivize workers to come up with more efficient ways to do their jobs. The worker will get a portion of the cost savings if their creative ideas save the company money. Jobs should also be challenging. Some jobs, such as neurosurgery, are inherently challenging and others such as factory-line work will be less so. Employers can still facilitate challenge in line work by having employees occasionally switch jobs or they can offer new training.

New education and training allows for development. Many employers pay for employees to get another degree or acquire new skills. The Pointy-Haired Boss doesn't really want people to develop at work. He just wants people to do their current job and honor new requests. In one *Dilbert* comic, the Boss says, "How is your employee engagement coming along?" Dilbert answers, "I'll make you a deal . . . I'll pretend I am happy here and you will pretend to believe it." The Boss cautions, "I need more than that. I also want you to pretend you are loyal to the company." Dilbert replies, "I can do that if you pretend you are interested in my career development," to which Boss asks, "Can we do that without talking?" Dilbert says, "It's best that way." The comic ends with Boss saying, "My job was a lot harder before I learned all the shortcuts." Development opportunities must be real and not just a name change. The Boss gave Asok a promotion once and said, "Your new title is spelled the same as the old title, but the pronunciation is totally different."

Honesty is also important. Jobs, which force a person to lie will corrupt a person's character. The virtue of honesty can be lost, and the employee tends to feel as bad as the person receiving the lie. Jobs that require lying are dirty jobs. In one *Dilbert* strip, Boss cautions, "Stop being honest when you go on sales calls." Dilbert asks, "You want me to lie?" Boss responds, "I would never ask you to lie. I am asking you to nod your head and smile while our salesperson lies." Adams knows that structures built to encourage lying may harm both sales and salespeople in the long term. The employees at Wells Fargo, who were forced to set up additional fake accounts for current customers to meet sales quotas, likely didn't jump for joy for their achievements.

Schumacher also includes beauty as a job requirement, a criterion that Adams cleverly shows is missing in most corporate jobs. The drab cubicle office is an ugly hell that most workers must stare into eight to ten hours a day. Tina informs the staff of the office relocation, "Your new cubicles will be a color called 'Death Eater Gray.' The fabric is a soul sponge that will absorb your happiness if you stand near it." Later the boss asks, "How'd the meeting go?" Tina replies, "Well, you know, fear of the unknown." Beauty may be hard to define, but some situations show its obvious absence.

The human fulfillment model does have its problems. It is unclear how many jobs can incorporate honesty, creativity, beauty, and love. How does a job pumping out port-a-johns involve beauty and goodness? Some work just needs to get done even though it's no one's calling in life. Other jobs, such as assembly-line work, lack creativity ninety-nine percent of the time. In addition, some people don't want jobs that require creativity. Some people like boring, monotonous jobs. Other employees may forsake beauty on the job for higher pay. They don't mind a nondescript beige cubicle. The job pays better and smells better than their last job, cleaning the locker rooms at the gym. The question of what kind of job best fits your life should mostly be left up to the free choice of the employee. The classical model of work didn't identify the importance and impact of work on our lives. The human fulfillment model too narrowly defines what good work must look like.

Flying Free with a Net

The Kantian middle view of work holds that people should be free to decide what work best fits their idea of a good life within a moral framework. You can pick a blue- or white-collar job, you can choose to sell or produce, manage or follow. Whatever job or career you select, there must be worker protections to make sure the employee isn't unjustly used. Every job must have a minimum wage, a safe work environment, freedom to assemble, and a culture of honesty. This view is also a middle ground when it comes to a work ethic. We should work hard, but not too hard. Leisure and work are both important to a meaningful life. Finding a good balance is important and the right balance can differ depending upon individual abilities and interests.

This theory differs from the classical view, because it holds that work can be intrinsically good and that work is a major element of meaning in people's lives. Gini is right that our careers are central to our identities as persons. The theory differs from the human fulfillment model, because there is not a uniform set of criteria that every job must have for people to reach their full potential. We can even imagine Sisyphus having a meaningful life if he truly enjoys rolling the rock each day up the hill and is satisfied with his achievement each night afterwards.

According to Kant, our ability to act freely on the basis of reasons is what makes us moral creatures. Humans are able to make intentional choices. When we use someone as a mere means, we are treating her as an object that lacks free will and rationality. Respect recognizes the subject as a moral being. Adams's characters often feel like they are being used. One example is when the CEO made the intern Asok drink the industrial sludge at a press conference, in order to show it was safe. A day later Dilbert says, "It lopped a few points off of his IQ, but he still has a bright future in quality assurance or maybe marketing. And with his new tail he'd be an awesome zip line guide." No matter what level of work, physical and mental health are necessary to achieve whatever end a person chooses.

The Kantian model maintains that employers should strive to make work meaningful, just not to the extent of the human fulfillment model. Work must allow for people to find meaning, both in and outside work. Employers need not bring high levels of values, such as creativity and beauty, into every job. Yet, they must not rob people of their physical and mental health, and they must allow people to be moral.

Norman Bowie, a modern day Kantian, says that there must be a "moral minimum" in place to ensure workers are not abused. A moral minimum is missing at Dilbert's workplace. A proud culture of deceit and contempt persists. As we saw, the boss says he can't order Dilbert to lie, and yet there are pressures and structures in place that require it. Dilbert is caught in what anthropologist Gregory Bateson calls a "double bind," where there are two schizophrenic messages that contradict each other.

Proponents of the classical view of work might reply that even this view requires too much of employers and employees. The costs are too high for employers to make jobs meaningful. Also, as Adams points out, we don't want our physician or pilot to get creative to spice up her job. Finally, if an employee is willing to accept greater pay for lower safety standards or worse treatment, shouldn't she be allowed to make that trade-off? In an open and free economy, employees are free to quit one job and take another.

The Kantian can reply to each of these concerns. First, the Kantian model is a moderate one and hence the costs are not as high as would be found in the human fulfillment model. Following the moral minimum might even have the side effect of being profitable for companies. Adams has an economic theory that says that happiness creates money. He believes that employees should not focus on making money directly. They should focus on their own happiness and money will follow. Happy people work harder and better. Employers should focus on this too. A more casual dress and work environment that is standard in much of Silicon Valley is part of this approach as well as features such as sleep pods that allow for a rejuvenating nap.

Second, doctors and pilots generally are not creative, but we want them to be when unique bad scenarios occur. Adams maintains that there is good and bad creativity. Squashing it all would get rid of the good as well bad. Third, it's often difficult for employees to find another job. Economic conditions and family situations are a couple of the reasons that employees often cannot just jump to another more meaningful job. Finally, employees do need to be protected from bad decisions. The greater psychological salience of short term benefits might cloud their ability to consider longer term harms, and they are often simply unaware of potentially negative long term consequences. Unsafe work conditions could take years to cause the resultant harms, and the first generation will suffer the consequences before the word gets out. The Kantian view stresses that paying someone a good salary doesn't mean that the person can be treated as a mere means.

Respecting a person involves recognizing their free will and their ability to create a meaning life at work and beyond. These are courtesies generally missing in the world of *Dilbert*. The Pointy-Haired Boss and Wally treat each other terribly, and as Adams points out, this is probably because they don't respect themselves. Treating others with respect seems to be a necessary condition for respecting yourself and living a meaningful life. When Boss says, "Alice you should act if you're your own boss," Alice replies, "Okay. My hair is pointy and I am confused. Suddenly, I have no respect for myself. Must golf now." Boss says, "That's so not funny."

Good Work

So, what is good work? Good work respects people's freedom and intelligence. Good work protects people's capabilities. And good work pays a sufficient wage to allow for meaning outside of work. Work is essential for living a meaningful life. Adams reminds us in his books and in *Dilbert* how important it is to treat people with respect in the workplace. Through characters such as robots, animal humans, various bosses, vulnerable interns, Wally, Alice, and Dilbert himself, we're reminded that all people deserve recognition and respect. Work must get done and orders must often be followed, but a moral minimum must be in place for trust and meaning to exist.

Employees then should search for work that they love. They should seek work that inspires, and environments that promote their creativity and worth as intelligent human beings. They should do the opposite of Wally, while keeping his insightful eye on corporate bullshit. Ideally, Gini says that we need to find our labor of love. That is the work we do not because we are paid for it but because of the satisfaction it provides.

Pay is necessary to live, and meaningful work is necessary for really living.

V

Golden Age, Ready or Not

15
Bias Is Rational!

RAY SCOTT PERCIVAL

What a piece of work is man! How noble in reason! How infinite in faculty! In form and moving how express and admirable! In action how like an angel! In apprehension how like a god!

—*Hamlet*, Act II, scene 2

Scott Adams feels that he must convince us that people are irrational, at least ninety percent of the time. People are under the influence of unconscious biases and prejudices. These biases are not reached by a process of intellectual justification, but are either installed by evolution, conditioned, or "spontaneously hallucinated." He tells us that

If we could accept that humans are fundamentally irrational, we could program ourselves for higher levels of happiness and productivity than we currently enjoy. (Posted on Adams's Blog, June 10th 2010, in #General Nonsense)

What, according to Adams, are the main biases?

A good general rule is that people are more influenced by visual persuasion, emotion, repetition, and simplicity than they are by details and facts. (*Win Bigly*, p. 25)

Adams's view of biases is part of his Moist Robot Hypothesis: humans are living creatures without free will, determined by certain stimuli and a set of biases, not by truth or logic. Simplicity, repetitive messages, flags, monuments, and emotionally stirring rallies dominate the masses.

But as we'll see, the Moist Robot Hypothesis is wrong. The biases of visual propaganda, emotion, repetition, and simplicity are perfectly rational. You'll also be relieved to know that you're not a robot.

The Science of Bias

Adams is heavily influenced by the modern science of biases. The theory that people are fundamentally irrational has dominated Western thinking for over one hundred years, and it is continually restated afresh by popular writers. A recent major advocate of this popular theory is Daniel Kahneman.

Kahneman is currently the king of bias research. His bestselling book *Thinking, Fast and Slow*, portrays people as unwittingly under the sway of biases, challenging the assumption often made by economists that people make rational choices. Kahnemann's experimental results are fascinating. Kahnemann's interpretation of these results is that we have two cognitive systems: an inaccurate, fast one (System 1), and a slow, effortful, more accurate, reflective one (System 2). Kahneman, most of the time, is careful in his presentation and is reserved about calling people "irrational," but those who refer to his work are often less cautious.

Typically, popularizers of bias research will set up an unrealistic, godlike idea of what it is to be rational, such as acting in the light of all relevant information, or the known optimal amount of data, or being perfectly logically coherent, or ignoring irrelevant information—and then celebrate how stupid we all are by contrast.

For a flavor of this approach, take a look at some of the titles of the myriad books published in this vein: *Predictably Irrational: The Hidden Forces that Shape Our Decisions* (Ariely, 2009), *Sway: The Irresistible Pull of Irrational Be-*

havior (Brafman and Brafman, 2008); *Kluge: The Haphazard Construction of the Human Mind* (Marcus, 2008). Evidently people just love being told how idiotic they are by psychologists, philosophers, and journalists.

Research into bias ought to be applauded. However, most bias researchers, in their conclusions, like to stress that we don't arrive at our conclusions by reasoned argument from "relevant information" (System 2), but instead that we are under the unconscious influence of our biases and prejudices (System 1).

One type of supposedly irrational bias is the so-called "anchor" phenomenon, sometimes famously utilized by Donald Trump. Someone enters a negotiation with a figure (any figure). The subsequent bargaining will typically gravitate toward that figure, even though no one has propounded a logically reasoned justification for it. The anchor is merely adduced. It may even be influenced by what the researchers call "irrelevant information." For example, if a potential buyer of an expensive yacht is exposed to an earlier conversation on a completely different (irrelevant) topic to very high prices, that buyer will be disposed to accept a higher price for the yacht than they would otherwise. Typically, this is seen as showing that people are irrational and closed to, or at least disproportionately insensitive to, argument. Adams shares this irrationalist view:

> An anchor is a thought that influences people toward a persuader's preferred outcome. For example, a big opening demand in a negotiation will form a mental anchor that will bias negotiations toward that high offer. (*Win Bigly*, p. 27)

Adams explains that this is due to a more general inclination of the mind to accept the first position it encounters. He also says that this then becomes almost impervious to argument:

> The human brain forms a bias for the things it hears first. If we accept the thing we hear first, it tends to harden into an irrational belief. And then it is difficult to dislodge. If your friends are reinforcing the idea too, it becomes hard as steel. (*Win Bigly*, p. 111)

Biases Are Heuristics

Not all psychologists are believers in the irrationality of biases. Gerd Gigerenzer, director of the Center for Adaptive Behavior and Cognition (ABC) at the Max Planck Institute for Human Development, is one of Kahneman's main critics. Gigerenzer argues that biases are useful rules of thumb—heuristics. When confronted by an avalanche of information, a heuristic is a simple tool of thought that gets you to a solution faster and more efficiently than a more reflective, fuller calculation might. Sometimes less is more. A heuristic can be either conscious or unconscious.

Contrary to Kahneman, Gigerenzer emphasizes that often your intuitive thoughts (System 1) are both faster and more accurate. Think of the problem faced by a baseball player trying to catch a ball. The full calculation of the trajectory of the ball from hit to its landing point, would outstretch the capacity of contemporary supercomputers. But baseball players don't do it that way. To catch a ball that's already in flight, they follow this rule of thumb: fix your gaze on the ball, start running and adjust your speed so that the angle of gaze remains constant. You can see that players aren't calculating the full trajectory of the ball, which would include where the ball will land, because the players often run into walls in pursuit of the ball. Apparently, many players apply this heuristic unconsciously, while others are aware of it and can formulate it.

Gigerenzer has discovered a plethora of these rules of thumb that we tailor to the right circumstances. Another bias is the so-called "recognition heuristic." Suppose you're asked which city has the larger population: Detroit or Milwaukee. Gigerenzer found that ignorance is an advantage here. He found that when he asked a class of American college students this question, forty percent got the answer right. But when he asked an equivalent class of German students, who knew next to nothing about these cities, the same question, all of them got the right answer: Detroit. The German students, undistracted by lots of details about the two cities, used the intuition: if you recognize the name of only one of two cities, that one will likely have the larger population.

Biases can be adaptive to our circumstances. Gigerenzer calls this "ecological rationality." Gigerenzer's work strongly suggests that biases are things we can work with, despite their using much less than the theoretical maximum amount of information. It was accepted for a long time that there is always a trade-off between speed and accuracy of solution. That's why Kahneman's System 1 is often thought to be fast but inaccurate. However, as Gigerenzer has shown, you can get both speed and accuracy from a simple heuristic, an unconscious bias. In addition, when faced by a complex problem, often a simple approach is better: a complex problem does not always require a complex solution.

Adams does, now and then, hint that we have to work with our biases, but he also, confusingly, asserts that they are irrational. Are we to surmise that perhaps this is Adams's anchor maneuver on rationality: come in with the outrageous claim that we are all ninety-percent irrational, wait for the attention, then soften up on the claim?

Rationality is not a matter of having no biases, nor is it a matter of arriving at your position by a process of justification. You are rational because your experience modifies your biases, or at least how you manage them. Far from being a hindrance, your biases and prejudices are vital to the process of improving your knowledge and adapting to your circumstances. Because biases are just a starting point, it doesn't matter where or how you got them. Therefore, even if you start a negotiation for the price of a yacht with a higher price than you otherwise would have done because you happened to hear a conversation involving very high prices, this does not stop you adapting your bargaining as you learn more.

Being Rational Encompasses Error

But what, in general, is it to be rational? What is it to be irrational? Surprisingly, for someone who uses these terms so frequently, Adams gives us no general account of rationality or irrationality. I'm not going to monopolize these words. But just so that you know where I'm coming from, I'd suggest, as a start, that we use "rational" as short-hand for having a propensity to adapt what you more or less guess are your means to your goals, abandoning what you conjecture to be unfeasible or uneconomic. These guesses can be conscious or unconscious. Being irrational would be failing to adapt your means or ends in response to any amount of counterevidence.

I think that people are rational in this sense. Excepting brain damage, genetic abnormalities, illness, and extreme physical obstacles, it's simply a myth that there are people who are absolutely impervious to adaptation under all circumstances. (The issue is more fully explored in my book *The Myth of the Closed Mind.*)

My sense of "rational" is closer to Gigerenzer's than it is to Scott Adams's or Daniel Kahneman's conception. It is rationality for mortals, down to Earth. It does not require perfect coherence or stability of preferences (although these may be goals for some people) or selfishness (a person's goals may be altruistic) or the absence of ignorance (perfect knowledge), or the absence of bias. However, unlike Gigerenzer, I lay fundamental stress on the conjectural nature of our grappling, stumbling attempts to master and understand the world, including the internal world of our own minds.

Rationality can encompass ignorance, error, and logical incoherence because rationality is a propensity to improve. Therefore, focusing on how ignorant and incoherent people are at any given point may cause us to overlook their ability to develop and grow.

In contrast, Adams implies that most of us are impervious to the facts, as his definition of anchoring suggests. There is a tradition of thought, of which Adams is part, which lays down impossible standards for rationality, and by these standards, it's easy to come up with examples of irrationality. Bias research has in many instances been swept along by this tradition of thought.

Knowing Newton's Ocean

My counterclaim is that people, despite appearances, are prone to be rational in possibly the most important sense. We have a propensity to produce ideas and beliefs spontaneously and abandon our beliefs in the light of contrary evidence. This idea of rationality can encompass ignorance, error, and bias. How?

Gigerenzer has shown that biases are a way of adapting to the demands of your specific environment, providing in some cases accurate solutions to complex problems with simple heuristics while remaining ignorant of much of the relevant information. In the example of the recognition heuristic applied to the population size of cities, it only works because you are mostly ignorant of the cities. Gigerenzer's work shows how we cope in domains that we can at least set the boundary to: a baseball park, guesses about city populations, and so forth.

I go a little further than Gigerenzer: rationality can encompass bias, ignorance, and error in the domain of absolute uncertainty, where we can't even define the likely boundary of the realm of the unknown. This is right up Scott Adams's street: beyond the edge of the parochial "known" to the unfathomable reality that Adams claims we are not equipped to even hint at. However, in contrast to Adams, I'm suggesting that we can make fruitful forays into the unknown, even if fully exploring the unknown is an infinite task.

We're all governed by unjustified biases, we're infinitely ignorant, and we're always prone to systematic errors. However, we can correct our mistakes and even arrange circumstances to adjust for our biases. That's why we can then make indefinite progress in our knowledge, technology, and civilization. That's the real and defensible meaning of the Shakespeare quotation.

Adams, along with much bias research, underestimates the problem of knowing the world, an economic problem that, like all economic problems, takes time. Adams himself continually reminds us how much training and time it takes to become a Master Persuader or a trained hypnotist. Nevertheless, elsewhere, Adams dramatizes error by saying that we frequently "hallucinate" things. But making mistakes, even systematically, is not irrational. Everyone confronts a world that is not just mostly unknown to them but infinitely beyond their grasp. Anyone's grasp! Forever!

As Isaac Newton put it:

> I do not know what I may appear to the world, but to myself I seem to have been only like a boy playing on the seashore and diverting myself in now and then finding a smoother pebble or a prettier shell than ordinary, whilst the great ocean of truth lay all undiscovered before me. (Brewster, *Memoirs*, Volume II, Chapter 27)

Being rational in such a world, then, has to be a more modest, but powerful, propensity: trial and error, being open to changing our beliefs in response to the discovery of error.

Rationality for humans cannot consist of acting without bias on all the relevant or even the known optimal amount of information. Only a god could do that. Adams is right there: we're not gods. However, Newton wasn't suggesting that we're confined to the beach. I think he's better understood as suggesting that the business of knowing the world is an infinite task. You can sail out into Newton's unknown ocean by trial and error, eliminating your errors as you go, replacing them by better trials, better ideas.

Experience Is Full of Theories

Not that you can get ahead of your judgment—even our experience is laden with theory. That's one thing that Adams gets right: that two groups of people can be "watching two different movies on the same screen." Your mind is constantly trying to get a good fit between its sensory input and its "movie." You can see this at work in the visual illusion of the sketch that seems to change from a sketch of a rabbit to one of a duck and back again. The sketch fits both interpretations,

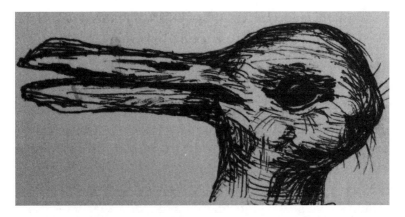

so your visual system vacillates between the two. Make a small change to the sketch, and the illusion evaporates.

The same is true of your beliefs. The "movies" may flip, as with abandonment of the delusion that Trump was the next Hitler. Adams says this! So, what's the point in calling people irrational? None.

Baby Scientist and Her Dog Defeat Moist Robot

We're wired from birth both to jump to conclusions and to revise those conclusions. Babies actively make exploratory guesses about how the world works and then revise those guesses in the light of experience. Alison Gopnik's research demonstrates that babies learn like scientists. Babies start with questions or problems, produce guesses, have these guesses refuted, replacing them with different and better guesses.

The human infant is thrust into the world already armed with rudimentary expectations or theories about the world and actively tries to impose them. But the world kicks back. Recalcitrant experiences then modify the expectations, and better expectations or theories then replace these. Alison Gopnik elaborates this view in her book, *The Scientist in the Crib*.

Adams has adopted the popular theory of human irrationality that became prominent at the end of the nineteenth century. Gustave Le Bon popularized the theory that the masses think in logically disconnected series of images and are moved by sheer affirmation, not logic.

> Affirmation pure and simple, kept free of all reasoning and all proof, is one of the surest means of making an idea enter the mind of the crowds. (*The Crowd*, p. 77)

Le Bon was opposed to democracy. A few discerning scholars and intellectuals might be capable of rational deliberation, but not the masses, controlled by their emotions and biases. Adolf Hitler's ideas on how to persuade the masses, expressed in *Mein Kampf*, are indebted to Le Bon.

Building on Le Bon, and trying to explain the popularity of fascism, Sergei Chakhotin later added Pavlov's theory that we are just a complex set of reflexes. The socialist Chakhotin believed that the experience of fascism had shown how intellectuals could scientifically control the minds of the unintellectual and emotional masses. The visual propaganda of flags, symbols, monuments, and emotionally stirring rallies dominated the masses, and could be used scientifically by the left.

Here we see the background of Scott Adams's concept of irrationality. In Pavlov's theory, because a stimulus such as a bell has reliably preceded the receipt of food by a dog, eventually the dog starts to salivate before it receives food, on merely hearing the bell. The dog's salivation has been "conditioned" to the bell. If the bell no longer precedes the food, the conditioned salivation reflex is extinguished. This is the pedigree of the so-called "Moist Robot Hypothesis."

Pundits of the Moist Robot Hypothesis seem unaware that not only Pavlov's theory but also the whole idea of reducing mental life to associations—the philosophy of associationism—is now refuted and defunct psychology. An extreme version is "the blank slate," the theory that we enter the world with an empty mind. Less extreme views, such as Pavlov's, allow us some innate tendencies specific to our species, but stimuli are supposed to determine the expression of these instincts. Not to worry, though! Adams allows you at least sex, love, and romance.

There are alternative approaches. One of them goes back to nineteenth-century psychologists such as Otto Selz of the Wurzburg school, who discovered that we don't think solely in terms of images or associations, but instead of networks of "directed thoughts" and attempts to solve problems. Independently, Karl Popper came to a similar conclusion, that expectations precede experience, and he put forward the general schema: Problem 1 → Tentative Theory → Error elimnation → Problem 2. Experience enters the picture, not by forming associations or conditioned reflexes, but by modifying pre-existing expectations by surprise and disappointment.

Pavlov's dogs and Gopnik's babies are actively searching for regularities in their world, important for their goals and values, and they create trial expectations or theories. These are modified, and the baby and dog settle, for the time being, on an expectation of food and a new toy in the presence of the bell sound (or mother's voice), enabling them to prepare for food (or play). When the bell (or voice) no longer presages food (or new toy), the expectation of food (or new toy) is refuted.

But the baby and the dog, busy exploring the world and attempting to answer their questions, often interrupt the attempt to "condition" them. If something novel happens, the baby stops smiling, and the dog no longer salivates, while they explore the novel event. Pavlov noticed this behavior in dogs but insisted on calling it a "reflex" anyway. The marketing guru Robert Cialdini, author of *Pre-Suasion* and whom Adams has admiringly nicknamed the "Godzilla" of influence, follows Pavlov in this when referring to the so-called "orienting reflex." We've all experienced this "orienting reflex," in TV ads with a barrage of shortcuts each shouting, "Look here!"

Thus, due to the innate bias of the human mind to understand the world, you end up producing a network of biases, intuitions, prejudices that frame your view of the world. These biases are your indispensable guide to life, though they are not infallible and you may occasionally modify them.

Surviving Criticism

Science makes this innate tendency more formal, systematic, and powerful. Prompted by a problem, the scientist formulates competing theoretical conjectures about the world and then performs carefully controlled experiments to undermine them by confronting them with refuting observations. These conjectures, such as Einstein's idea that the speed of light is a constant, are leaps in the dark that solve the problem at hand. This is where I leave Gigerenzer's approach behind on the beach finding a prettier shell than ordinary. His ecological rationality, brilliant though it is, is confined to Newton's beach; any new knowledge, including new heuristics, is to be found in deep water. In this case there is nothing else for it: you have to take a plunge into the unknown.

Outside of science, where observational criticism may be hard to come by, the critic uses other standards against which to test the proposed idea, such as self-coherence and consistency with less problematic theories that do have observational tests. You can arrive at a true position, but only tentatively and without justification. The key is the invention of systematic methods to test our theories and even our very methods. This is the reputable method proposed by Karl Popper, critical rationalism. Of course, it's a controversial philosophical view of how we gain knowledge, and I'm only dropping a hint about it. But it's healthy to have some competition in ideas.

On the old conception of rationality, even criticism was defined as showing that a view lacks justification. But if justification is not feasible, then criticism has to be understood as confronting a position with a mismatch between it and some objective standard—one that can be publically tested systematically by some method. Instead of proving that our theory is true, we settle for showing that it has survived attempts to prove it wrong. It looks true, it approximates the truth better than anything else we know, and it might even be true.

Battle of the Biases

Critical rationalism provides the tools crucial to rooting out our unconscious biases: competing theories expressed in language plus public testability. When we compare and test different theories, views, doctrines, and ideologies, our unconscious presuppositions and biases become conscious, placed on the slab for dissection. But we do need the liberty to express our biases without hindrance from such things as PC-speak or ministries of fake news. We need a battle of the biases. I rather suspect that Adams would agree with this.

From this perspective, it is irrelevant where and how you came by your bias or prejudice. Whether you got it by consulting tealeaves, from a marijuana trip, bumping your head, hearing the speech of a charismatic leader at an emotionally charged rally while gazing at a beloved flag, having it repeated to you in a simple advertisement, or having your brain spontaneously produce it, the question is: can you correct it by critical argument? You can also see that simple assertion ("affirmation") is completely legitimate. It is a conjecture.

My view puts biases in a radically different light. Take the anchor bias. When someone enters a negotiation with a figure (an anchor), even without a certificate of justification, it is still something you can work with, correcting it according to your own guesses and counterargument. You may even have to invent new standards or techniques for testing the hypotheses, to see if you can find a mismatch.

Emotion, the Badass of Biases

According to Adams, "When our feelings turn on, our sense of reason shuts off" (p. 45), and "People don't change opinions about emotional topics just because some information proved their opinion to be nonsense. Humans aren't wired that way" (*Win Bigly*, p. 61).

It's common to divide our mental life into a reasoning or rational self, governed by logic and inference and an emotional self, ruled by instinctual or habitual emotion. When I'm admiring my national flag or getting excited watching my local football team, I'm driven by passion. When I'm striving to get a good grade in my SATs, I'm using reason. However, the Stoics, the ancient Greek philosophers who founded logic, refuted this view more than two thousand years ago.

The problem with the division between an emotional self and a rational self is that all emotion is thoughtful and all thought is emotional. Even the "unemotional" intellectual thoughts of the scientist are filled with feelings, perhaps feelings of curiosity and wonder. A woman walking down the street sees a man grab hold of a woman and violently throw her to one side. She is angry with the man and runs over to protest, only to find that the man was protecting the woman from tiles falling from a roof in the wind. (*She interprets her experience through a theory, which is promptly refuted.*) Her anger rapidly changes to admiration and relief. (*Her old theory is replaced by a new one, creating new emotions.*) And, she can't help herself changing her emotions in this way.

According to Adams's "filter" theory, this is not supposed to happen; she ought to continue berating or beating him senseless for his ungentlemanly behavior. But this is typical of emotions: what you feel partly depends on what you think, what you believe is fact. And belief is involuntary; you can't change your beliefs by an act of will. And because you don't choose your beliefs, you don't decide how you feel. You can't help re-checking your beliefs, moment by moment, even if your more fundamental values or goals remain more stable.

Oddly, Adams, I surmise, would agree with most of what I've said here. He even points out, in places, that biases may be useful as, for example, shortcuts in finding solutions. I can imagine him saying (though he hasn't actually said it), "It's better to have something to work with rather than nothing, better to have a biased mind than an empty mind."

Standing on the seashore of your infinite ignorance, you may adopt a critical but kinder attitude to your follies and flaws, which, to a god, are but foibles of the finite. Not only are you free to find prettier shells than ordinary; given some courage you may even find some bizarre creatures out in the deep.

Breathing in the fresh sea breeze, you may also feel free to embrace the exciting thought that, while you may be moist, you're no robot.

16
Why Scott Adams Is Stupid

Daniel Miori

In case the title didn't give it away, the purpose of this chapter is to take a swipe at Scott Adams. If you're a serious fan don't worry, he doesn't really care what's written here. As this book goes to press, Wikipedia says his net worth is $70 million. This little chapter certainly won't be putting a dent in that anytime soon. Additionally, by the Adams standard, that pot of money is proof that he's much smarter than everyone else—experts in their fields, contributors to this book, readers of this book, everyone.

The statement "Scott Adams is a smart man" is probably correct, but other than the fact that he is sitting on a small mountain of cash what proof do we have? He was valedictorian of his high school graduating class, but with only thirty-eight others in that class, it isn't as interesting as you might think. What we *know* is that he got better grades than thirty-eight other people his age. The same could be said for someone who graduated 462nd in a class of five hundred.

We *know* he has a master's degree from The University of California at Berkeley, which sounds good till you realize it's a Master's in Business Administration (MBA), often considered the rhinestone of graduate degrees, shiny but pretty much worthless. An informal survey of university faculty conducted for this chapter suggests that while there may be a few genuinely brilliant candidates in MBA programs, the majority simply have money in their pockets and a desperate craving for official recognition. Universities, even schools with good reputations like Berkeley, don't mind taking that money. It annoys the crap out of the faculty forced to teach the MBA classes, but it's way better than bake sales as a fund raiser.

Having initiated the requisite sarcasm and poking of fun, the genuine purpose of this chapter is to look at Adams's opinion of science and the scientific method, how he states those views, and to put that into a philosophical perspective. To keep this discussion manageable, it will be based on the following charitable and open-minded summary, which, in his own words, might sound like this:

- **I'm smarter than the experts.**

- **I'm a cartoonist, not a moralist.**

- **If you disagree with me it's because you aren't as smart as I am.**

- **If you build a better factual case, you are hysterical and that isn't what I said in the first place.**

- **If you argue that factual case better, then you misunderstand me entirely. I'm just a cartoonist and you lack a sense of humor, you don't get that I'm just kidding around.**

- **And finally, I'm smarter than the experts.**

As to how he states his views, basically he was the guy on the playground who would whisper, *"Tommy's mother might not be a whore, but all those guys who have sex with her leave money on her nightstand . . . I'm just sayin'."*

We will be looking at Adams's—let's call it—opinion on a few topics, but one which comes up often is the science of climate change. Note, however, this chapter will not seek to refute any position he may or may not take, that can easily be done with well referenced replies available on the internet, like Keith Pickering's "A Detailed Reply to Scott Adams on Climate Science," as well as easily accessible and very solid science, like the 2017 EPA report on climate change.

If you would like to break away quickly and read an example of his "writing," the post on his website from September 11, 2017 entitled "When to Trust the Experts (Climate and Otherwise)" should do. Spoiler alert, it's not about when to trust experts, it's about when not to trust experts that advance theories he doesn't like. If you don't want to read the post it's just as well, we will tumble along blissfully unencumbered by the facts, consistent with Adams's example.

To substantiate all these admittedly juvenile opinions, we'll review a sub-field of philosophy called epistemology; the philosophic concepts of empiricism, rationalism, and epistemic responsibility; and look at epistemic responsibility in research. Finally, as a bonus, we will unearth one of the great works of pseudo-science, *The Basic Laws of Human Stupidity*.

Epistemology

When we think of philosophers, most people picture a crazy old coot with poor hygiene who gives good life advice. The reality couldn't be farther from the truth. Philosophers are a conventional looking and diverse bunch who wash regularly and rarely, if ever, give good advice. It may seem like an arbitrary body of abstract ideas, but philosophy is a genuine attempt to better understand common human errors of belief and judgment. William James (1842–1910), a philosopher who is also regarded as the father of American psychology, called philosophy "a peculiarly stubborn effort to think clearly."

Epistemology is a major sub-field of philosophy and is concerned with the nature of knowledge. Not the kind of casual knowledge we all form every day, but with the understanding of what is actual and provable. For our purpose, it will be the difference between knowing and *knowing*. To *know* something requires you have a good reason, or *warrant*, for that belief. Having a *warrant* means both that you actually believe a thing to be true—you aren't just saying it to stir up trouble—and that you have proof that it is true. It's as though the philosophy cops were pounding on your door shouting, "We believe you are engaging in untruths!" and you get to say "Yes, but do you have a *warrant?*" Unless they have proof you're engaging in untruths, the philosophy cops have to stay outside. But, for the record, you might just as well open the door anyway, because philosophy cops are likely to break it down and kick your ass regardless.

Rationalism and Empiricism

Science and philosophy have more in common than you might think. Most science, like physics, math, and the logic that gave us computers, began as philosophical disciplines. Science has also had an impact on philosophy, affecting the way philosophers speak to each other. Two concepts in philosophy which describe how science works and how we gain knowledge are rationalism and empiricism.

Empiricism demands that we be certain of the accuracy of what we're saying. Just because we think something and believe it, doesn't mean that it's true. A strict empiricist would say that the warrant for a belief is more important than whether that belief was useful in explaining what has happened or in predicting things that will happen. Without that precise understanding of a situation, you can guess the right answer for the wrong reasons.

Adams infers that climate science lacks an *empiric* foundation, but he fails to even hint at where that lack of *empiric* understanding lay. Ludwig Wittgenstein (1889–1951), an advocate of empiricism in philosophy, believed that if you couldn't say something clearly and in a way which could not be misinterpreted, then you've failed to make your point and should just shut the hell up. He may not have said the "shut the hell up" part, but that tight-assed Austrian bastard was certainly thinking it.

Rationalism on the other hand, states that we can reason our way to an understanding of the world around us. Early rationalists felt that we were born with certain knowledge and that was why some people were smarter than others. The idea that we have been implanted with information before we were born has a strong suggestion of supernaturalism and has fallen out of favor, but having the ability to reason through something and come to an understanding of it without concrete evidence is a great description of how our brains work. Also, a rationalist would say that the (empiric) information our senses give us can be misinterpreted. Is the room dark or is the viewer suddenly blind? Therefore, rationalists aren't as strict as empiricists about what constitutes adequate *warrant*.

Epistemic Responsibility

William Clifford (1845–1879) was a mathematician and a philosopher of science. He was concerned that when scientists say they *know* something, it's because they worked hard at making sure it was accurate. It's called *epistemic responsibility*, and it is important to all of us. Good science is good because of this drive for accuracy and truth. We depend on it for medical treatment and airbags in cars and food that doesn't kill us. Of course, the methods necessary to provide epistemically responsible results are sometimes ignored—maybe due to ego or greed—but the concept itself is research bedrock.

Clifford tells us that whether harm from incorrectly held beliefs occurs or not, "It is wrong always and everywhere for anyone to believe anything upon insufficient evidence." He would go on to say that even if we did not share our unfounded conclusions with others—like in a blog or on YouTube, Twitter, or Periscope—people will be influenced by our wrongly-held beliefs through our actions, our words, or our comic strips (if by an off chance we are lucky enough to have any). He would say that it was not okay to bloviate about things you don't fully understand, things that you could *know* but choose not to, like climate change. He would tell Adams that his self-described habit of "sampling" television news is a terrible way to become informed and that he should either learn the science or *shut the hell up.* (Sorry about that last bit, Clifford had Wittgenstein's moxy but he was a Cambridge educated British gentleman and would never have said it. It was just fun to write.)

The Scientific Method

Karl Popper was a philosopher who began his career in the early twentieth century. He looked at the scientific figures of his day and saw two basic approaches. One was to propose a theory and then look for information which confirmed it, which was the way Sigmund Freud worked.

Despite Freud's having revolutionized the understanding of mental illness, this approach led Freud to make some very dubious claims about its nature. The problem is that when you have already decided your theory is true—like how women's problems are all due to their wanting a penis—it becomes easy to think you've found data which confirms it and to ignore data which might disprove it. This tendency is called *confirmation bias,* and it also happens to be one of Adams's favorite terms of abuse. He uses it like a club to attack opinions he disagrees with, despite his love for his own "predictive power." If one of Adams's theories appears to predict a future event, Adams takes that "predictive power" to be evidence that he's correct. If a theory opposed to Adams's view appears to predict future events, well now that would just be confirmation bias.

Falsifiability, Why Science Works

The other approach Popper looked at involves a thing called falsifiability, which isn't about telling fibs. It means that if an idea holds up to testing which could prove it false, then it must be good. Another scientist Popper was watching was Albert Einstein, who advanced his theories on physics and then waited for the results of experiments that could potentially disprove, or falsify, them. He was then able to revise the parts of his beliefs that were flawed, based on that new evidence. In a hundred years of attempts to refute Einstein's work, those theories have flexed somewhat but overall have held up remarkably well. Popper felt that *falsifiability* was the best way to improve knowledge. Many smart people agreed with him, and it has become the foundation of what we now consider good scientific method.

Criticisms of Falsifiability, Other than Adams

Paul Feyerabend (1924–1994), a philosopher of science, had a great deal to say that Adams might agree with. In his book *Against Method*, Feyerabend proposed, as Adams has also suggested, that language has limitations and even when scientists were being careful about how they described their findings, their use of language would be influenced by their beliefs. He argued against falsifiability as a single best method and instead offered an idea described as epistemological anarchy, where any method could be used for research provided it got results. Later in his career he softened his views and even completely reversed some of his argument against falsifiability, understanding that he may have simply provided an alternative that was novel, but was as restricting as he felt falsifiability to be.

Reproducibility

An important part of research is the idea that data gathered by one scientist should be reproducible by another scientist using the same method. One sign of epistemic responsibility in research today is the response to false claims made in high-profile studies, particularly in psychology and prescription drug research. Loose methods motivated by several things, including a desire to get published and, in big pharma, the need to move product, caused researchers to manipulate their findings to create the illusion of advances where there were none. Called the reproducibility crisis, it has created a drive for accountability among researchers and has caused greater scrutiny of research results in general, producing new systems to ensure that methods and data are standardized and made available for others to build on.

Adams points out that scientists jealously guard their data, which is true. It takes a lot of work and money to generate that information and no one wants to give it away; that would be like not licensing Dilbert and letting anyone profit from selling branded product. Websites like *Open Science Framework* establish structures for research methods as well as access to the data generated by other researchers. Adams is right that research has flaws, he is wrong to suggest that it's tolerated or to pass off the idea as if he's the only one who's noticed.

Mama Always Said, "Stupid Is as Stupid Does"

The Online Oxford English Dictionary tells us that *stupidity* is "Behavior that shows a lack of good sense or judgement." *Ignorance*, however, is defined as "Lacking knowledge or awareness in general; uneducated or unsophisticated." In other words, an ignorant person can behave intelligently, and an intelligent person can behave stupidly. Stupidity is not a natural state of being, it's the ability to make poor decisions despite your education or intelligence, just like Mama said.

In 1987, Carlo Cipolla, a Professor of Economics at Adams's alma matter UC Berkeley, who possibly even said some of those crappy things about MBAs earlier, wrote an article for the spring 1987 issue of the magazine *Whole Earth Review* titled *The Basic Laws of Human Stupidity*. It has achieved legendary status among academics because of his humorous and insightful thoughts on the nature of stupidity. It could even be considered good life advice since he was an economist, not a philosopher. Overall this is the kind of science-y stuff Adams should love, since it sounds right but isn't overly burdened with facts. All *rationalism*, no boring *empiricism*.

The laws are as follows:

I. Always and inevitably everyone underestimates the number of stupid individuals in circulation.

II. The probability that a certain person be stupid is independent of any other characteristic of that person.

III. A stupid person is a person who caused losses to another person . . . while himself deriving no gain and even possibly incurring losses.

IV. Non-stupid people always underestimate the damaging power of stupid individuals. In particular, non-stupid people constantly forget that at all times and places and under any circumstances to deal or associate with stupid people always turns out to be a costly mistake.

V. A stupid person is the most dangerous type of person.

In addition, Cippola offers the following four archetypes of behavior:

The intelligent person is someone who acts in ways that benefit both themselves and others. For example, a celebrity who actually learns a subject before writing about it.

The bandit acts in ways that benefits themselves but causes a loss to others. Say, a cartoonist who shills crap business advice on his website.

A helpless person acts in ways that cause a loss to themselves while producing a gain to another. Say, the consumer who buys that crap business advice.

Lastly and most importantly, the stupid person acts in ways that will cause a loss to themselves while causing a loss to others. For example, a cartoonist who lacks epistemic responsibility contributes to a deterioration in public discourse by posting his half-assed opinion on the Internet and as a result suffers a loss in income and reputation. Stupid.

Why Is Scott Adams Dangerous?

Calling it a day by using Cippola to say Adams is dangerous (Adams = stupid = dangerous) seems satisfying, and it's certainly consistent with Adams's methods, but it lacks a bit of that old epistemic responsibility, so here goes. Scott Adams is dangerous because of shoddy methods, a lack of integrity (disingenuously making then backing away from claims he can't support), greed, and he has a stupid face.

Well, maybe not because of his stupid face, but the other things definitely, and here's why.

Shoddy Methods

Volume volume volume! It may be a great way to keep prices low but saying many things in a poorly defined and emotional way is the opposite of how human understanding advances. Adams's speaking on multiple topics in a nearly constant stream makes holding him responsible for any specific idea impossible. His discussion is about winning, not about content. The advantage to argument in volume is that you never have to say you're sorry. If you get caught in your flawed argument you just go back to that other thing you said that sounded relatively less wrong.

Subjective use of words and terms. The list is long, confirmation bias, mass hysteria, cognitive dissonance, such as his August 17th 2017 blog line "A mass hysteria happens when the public gets a wrong idea about something that has strong emotional content and it triggers cognitive dissonance that is often supported by confirmation bias."

That sounds like ten pounds of manure in a five-pound bag because it is. When you say one thing as precisely and simply as possible you take responsibility for your idea. While that means you may have to revise your theory as better information becomes available, it also means you get to be intelligent. When you weasel your way out of admitting a mistake you stay trapped in your stupidity. One specific example is his abuse of the word *"persuasion"* (his italics). Another word which better describes his intended meaning would be *inveigle*, which is defined as to "Persuade (someone) to do something by means of deception or flattery." In fact, *coerce* might be the best choice when we consider just how often he tries to elicit an emotional response, usually on the way to pitching his latest product.

Lacking Integrity in His Approach

Feyerabend may have been a dope when he was running around Berkeley in the 1960s spouting his epistemic anarchy crap, but he took responsibility for his ideas and ate a great deal of criticism along the way. Also, he was able to revise his theories when they proved less effective at offering a real alternative to falsifiability.

Adams may have read Feyerabend; he may have heard about him second hand while at Berkeley; its remotely possible that Adams is so genuinely intelligent that the ideas simply occurred to him. The difference is that Adams doesn't propose and defend his theories so much as he suggests and retreats. His shallow and selective treatment of complex topics means that whatever valuable message may have been possible gets lost. Despite having knowledge from education and life experience, and despite having the resources to do so, Adams fails to become the educator and advocate that he could be.

It's All About the Benjamins

Nearly every blog post and web appearance ends by referring the reader to his NEW BOOK, ON SALE NOW!!! It is the one constant and unifying aspect of his Internet presence. Although opening a discussion of the morality of advertising as provocateur is beyond this chapter, it certainly adds perspective to his science-bashing, he's just trying to move some product.

It's not Scott Adams's fault that people are interested in every stupid thing celebrities say. Also, this is a free market economy, and barring a Marxist revolution, he can use whatever guerilla advertising he likes. Unfortunately, disparaging the scientific method and the process of research goes beyond advertising, since doing so could not significantly contribute to his bottom line.

Research provides us with the best options available given the knowledge and resources we have. The process isn't always perfect, the advice experts give is not always one hundred percent right, but perhaps one of the miracles of science done correctly is that the advice is nearly always pretty darn good. Climate science, medicine, engineering, and every other field we stake our lives on every day is a chaotic mix of information, understanding, and probability. Accepting this fact is one part of our human experience that many of us are fortunate enough to ignore every day. In many parts of the world people are impacted by climate instability and its man-made causes, but they don't have the luxury of debating it over coffee. They're just trying to live through the day. We have the privilege to consider it and should.

Ultimately the question you should ask yourself is this, do you want your doctor to treat you like Scott Adams does? If you don't mind being talked out of proven therapies and being *persuaded* into some snake oil treatment that he couldn't take the time to understand but will profit from, please buy into Adams's skewed view of science and research. If you'd rather depend on the honest opinion of an experienced, well informed, and well-trained professional, then it's possible you may agree that Scott Adams is stupid to undercut science and research just to sell some product, and that he's dangerous.

Finally, it's clear that Adams is trying to make with the funny, but he fails. He fails because he could be intelligent, benefiting himself and others, but can't quite seem to grasp it. He fails because his main motivation is to make money, incurring a loss to others; and because he is unable to establish any *warrant* for his views, incurring a loss to whatever good reputation he may have had. His self-professed ability to *know* things without *warrant* shows rationalism without the empiricism to balance it, seemingly because his gut tells him so.

Dilbert might reply to that claim, as he did to his pointy haired boss in an October 2017 strip, "I'm curious, where do you stick your head to listen to your gut?" Samuel Clemens couldn't make the funny when he became obsessed with attacking the Christian Science movement; Lenny Bruce couldn't when his act got bogged down in his court battles; and if those actual humorists couldn't be funny after losing their way, then you can be damn sure Adams can't. Stay in your lane, Scott, keep drawing your funny pictures, cash those checks, and shut the fuck up about the rest.[1]

---

[1] Cipolla's *The Basic Laws of Human Stupidity* is real but has sadly been out of print for some time, the copy used for this chapter was a PDF of a Xerox of the original. It's hard to find but well worth the effort, even if just for the underground-comix-style illustrations.

17
Sweeping Up God's Debris

RACHEL ROBISON-GREENE

Scott Adams's book *God's Debris* is an entertaining romp through the familiar terrain of some basic issues in philosophy. The premise is charming—a young man shows up to deliver a package and finds that, in fact, the package has delivered *him*. It brought him to the house of a man who we learn, in due course, is an *avatar*—a being that has reached the fifth and highest level of awareness that a human can achieve.

In the final pages of the book, we learn (spoiler alert) that at any given time, there can be only one avatar, and that the package has delivered this humble postman to this particular house because he is destined to become the current avatar's successor. I'll refer to the book's two main characters as The Avatar and The Postman.

Adams concludes the introduction to the book by prescribing to readers, "For maximum enjoyment, share *God's Debris* with a smart friend and then discuss it while enjoying a tasty beverage." Well, crack one open and we'll have some fun assessing the philosophical details of the story.

Awareness Is about *Unlearning*

Even if you've never studied philosophy, it's likely that you've heard of Socrates. For a philosopher who never wrote anything, he's stunningly pervasive in pop culture. Those who know a little about the life of Socrates know that he was sentenced to death for corrupting the youth and for failing to honor the gods of his culture. What we know about Socrates, we largely know through the works of Plato. Socrates is the main character in Plato's dialogues.

When Socrates pleads the case for his life in Plato's *Apology,* he offers the story of how he came to be widely regarded as wise. A friend of his, Chaerephon, visited the Oracle at Delphi. He asked the Pythian prophetess whether there was anyone wiser than Socrates, and she answered that there was no one wiser. After hearing this story, Socrates was confused because he knew he had no wisdom. He took pains to prove the prophetess wrong by consulting with a number of people reputed to be wise, but concluded mournfully that they were deluded about their own wisdom. He, among all the Greeks, was wisest because he alone knew that he knew nothing. He was aware of his own ignorance.

The old man to whom the unnamed protagonist in *God's Debris* delivers a package is a Socratic figure, and the method he uses throughout the story is the Socratic Method. Socrates was known in Athens as "the gadfly" for the tendency he had to flit about the city pestering people with questions. Most of Plato's dialogues feature Socrates in this role. He finds some unwitting citizen who claims to know something and then proceeds to thoroughly demonstrate that they actually have no idea what they are talking about. Within mere pages of *God's Debris*, the old man is off to the races, making deft use of the method of the most famous of the Greek philosophers. His approach isn't slow and steady— The Avatar is like Socrates on speed.

Near the conclusion of the book, The Avatar claims that there are five levels of awareness. The last is reserved for one and only one person—The Avatar himself. We'll discuss these five levels a little more later. The thing to focus on for our purposes at this point is that the process of reaching the fifth level is a matter of *unlearning*—of realizing just how much you don't know. So, in this sense, the Avatar is very Socratic.

The Avatar pushes The Postman to challenge his preconceptions about a stunning range of topics. To do justice to any of these topics would require a whole tome on each, so the goal here is not to settle each philosophical question once and for all. Rather, the goal, in very Socratic fashion, is to get The Postman to see just how much he *doesn't know.*

Introducing Global Skepticism

Though The Avatar is a Socratic figure, his approach also employs a dash or two of the methodology of a seventeenth-century French philosopher named René Descartes. Indeed, the story has the flavor of a book-length skeptical hypothesis exploring the possible gaps between what we seem to perceive and what reality is actually like.

Skeptical hypotheses are perhaps the philosophical concepts with which Hollywood is the most enamored; they appear in movies like *The Matrix, Inception, Vanilla Sky,* and *Total Recall.* Descartes offers two skeptical hypotheses in his *Meditations on First Philosophy.* Can Descartes know that he is *really* sitting in his chair, in front of a roaring fire, contemplating the extent of his knowledge?

Descartes considers the possibility that he may be dreaming an extremely realistic dream. If he were really in bed dreaming, everything would appear to him exactly the way it appears to him now, but all of the beliefs that he would form on the basis of those appearances would be false. He would, for example, falsely believe that he was sitting in front of the fire when he was actually snug in his bed.

The second skeptical hypothesis that he considers is that an evil demon is deceiving him, causing him to believe, in error, all of the things that he believes. If that were the case, there would be very little, if anything that we would know for certain. I'll spare you the details, but, by the end of the *Meditations,* Descartes thinks he's found a solution to the problems for knowledge posed by his skeptical hypotheses. We'll see if there's a way out of the skeptical quagmire Adams has dumped us into.

The skeptical hypothesis proposed by the Avatar is a little more complicated than those considered by Descartes. The main, titular, idea is that we *are* God's Debris. In one section of the book, The Avatar and The Postman consider whether, in his omniscient, omnipotent state, anything could ever truly motivate God. God lacks nothing. It's hard to think of anything he might want or anything he might take to be a challenge. The Avatar concludes that the only thing that could truly motivate God—the only thing that would truly constitute a challenge for a being of God's type—is self-destruction. The Avatar proposes the idea that this self-destruction has already occurred and that we, and all of the rest of the material universe, are the dust created by the destruction of God.

This proposal is radical, but it does not yet constitute the skeptical hypothesis that I've been promising. To get this, we need his next, radical, claim. The way we perceive the world is an illusion. In fact, the universe is comprised of two and only two things: dust and probability. The "dust" is constituted by "the smallest elements of matter, many levels below the smallest things scientists have identified." On the topic of probability, as we'll see, what The Avatar has to say about that is a little odd. The Postman offers the response that I think most of us would be inclined to offer. He points to the tremendous body of knowledge that human beings have managed to amass, particularly in recent years. The Avatar responds by saying:

> Every generation of humans believed it had all the answers it needed, except for a few mysteries they assumed would be solved at any moment. And they all believed their ancestors were simplistic and deluded. What are the odds that you are the first generation of humans who will understand reality?

What about the fact that human beings have been able to achieve tremendous advances in science and technology? The fact that innovations actually *work* seems to lend some credibility to the idea that we *actually know things*—a lot more things than humans have known at earlier points in history. The Avatar responds by saying:

> Computers and rocket ships are examples of inventions, not of understanding. All that is needed to build machines is the knowledge that when one thing happens, another thing happens as a result. It's an accumulation of simple patterns. A dog can learn patterns. There is no "why" in those examples. We don't understand why electricity travels. We don't know why light travels at a constant speed forever. All we can do is observe and record patterns.

What's more, the Avatar claims that the theories we use to describe the world are incorrect. For example, he claims that the force that we call gravity really doesn't exist, or, rather, something altogether different is happening. He says:

> The universe looks a lot like a probability graph. The heaviest concentrations of dots are the galaxies and planets, where the force of gravity seems the strongest. But gravity is not a tugging force. Gravity is the result of probability . . . Reality has a pulse, a rhythm, for lack of better words. God's debris disappears on one beat and reappears on the next in a new position based on probability. If a bit of God-dust disappears near a large mass, say a planet, then probability will cause it to pop back into existence nearer to the planet on the next beat. Probability is highest when you are near massive objects. Or to put it in another way, mass is the physical expression of probability.

This proposal—that cause and effect don't really function in the way that we think that they do—would mean that human beings are dramatically wrong about *everything*. Skepticism about cause and effect must lead, if we're rational, to a general skepticism about science, since science can't get off the ground without the thesis that some events truly do *cause* other events.

This skeptical hypothesis plays a role in in The Avatar's Socratic interrogation of The Postman. If what The Postman is claiming is possible, then his reliance on the received truths of science is unjustified. He must begin his process of *unlearning*.

Considering Causation

The suggestion that the Avatar seems to be making is that we are always missing a "why"—some causal feature or factor that fundamentally explains the constant conjunction between two events. He postulates, by way of skeptical hypothesis, the thesis that we never directly observe this "why" because it doesn't actually exist. One event follows another event on the basis of probability alone.

It seems, though, that the "why" Adams is looking for is actually causation itself. We experience the world in one state, other factors are introduced, and then we observe the world in a second state. We never actually experience the event that is causation.

It may well be that this isn't really much of a problem at all. Perhaps, rather than balking at the idea that causation ever happens on the basis of the fact that we never experience it, we just need a fleshed-out account of what causation is. Once we have that, the fact that we don't experience causation may turn out to be no problem at all—certainly not a problem that should generate skepticism on a global scale. There are many theories of causation on offer; perhaps The Postman would do well to consider those first.

What's the Chance that God Is Made of Probability?

Perhaps the most striking feature of the cosmology Adams has described here is the unique way or ways in which he repeatedly uses the word "probability." In the passage about gravity, recall that Adams says that, "probability will cause" a piece of God dust "to pop back into existence nearer to the planet on the next beat."

It is odd to speak of probability as "causing" anything. It's a category mistake. Consider a standard case of probability—an example that Adams himself makes use of for a different purpose in the book—an ordinary coin flip. Whenever a person flips a coin, so long as the coin is a standard coin, we can describe the probability of each outcome—it has a fifty percent chance of landing heads up and a fifty percent chance of landing tails up. Adams often speaks of probability as if it is an entity with causal powers. But when we describe the way the coin will land, we're simply describing the chances that the future (with respect to the coin) will turn out either of two particular ways. Probability itself is not an entity or an event. At best, probability is a feature of an event.

This is not the only occasion in which he speaks of probability in a non-standard way. When describing God, Adams has The Postman paraphrase The Avatar's revelation in the following way, "So you're saying that God—an all powerful being with a consciousness that extends to all things across time—consists of nothing but dust and probability?"

Again, Adams is treating the notion of probability here as if it has some special status on its own—as if it is itself an entity that can serve as one of the building blocks of God. We have another category mistake on our hands. Consider the case of a human person. We can describe the things a person consists of in a number of ways. We can say, for example, that Joe consists of muscles, organs, skin, and bone. We can say that he consists of various combinations of atoms, electrons, and protons. What we cannot say, for example, is that Joe consists of tallness. We can't say this, even if Joe is, in fact, tall. To do so would be a category mistake. Tallness is not something Joe is made of. Instead, it is a way of describing Joe, a way that turns out to be highly context-dependent. Joe may be tall relative to others who work at his office, but not tall relative to members of a professional basketball team or to a skyscraper.

Probability and tallness have something in common. Both can be used to describe things—events or states of affairs in the case of probability and objects or entities in the case of tallness. Neither tallness nor probability can be things that an entity "consists" in. We might say, in defense of The Avatar's view here, that God is a being unlike any other that we know. Perhaps God, as a non-physical, supernatural thing, could be made out of probability.

How is it that an all-good, all-powerful, all-knowing God who is an eternal, non-physical being can be fractured into two parts he didn't contain originally? If he were non-physical to begin with, how could he rupture into physical parts in the form of the dust of which the entire universe is comprised? How could an eternal God ever have been made of probability to begin with? Why would probability be part of the flotsam and jetsam of God's destruction?

The notion that God is non-physical or that God is omnipotent can't do anything to make it more likely that God could "consist of probability." A category mistake is a category mistake and, like the laws of logic, even an omnipotent God can't change that. Even an omnipotent God can't be made of "hate for Mondays" or "late for work." Those simply aren't the kinds of things beings can be made of. The same is true of probability.

Level Four or Level Five?

The Avatar claims that there are five basic levels of human awareness, and most people only reach three, four if they're lucky. The first level is self-awareness—the basic sense of awareness that you exist. At the second level of awareness, people understand that other people exist. In the third level of awareness, people realize that they may be wrong about some things, but are able to maintain their system of beliefs even in light of that recognition. The fourth level of awareness is what Adams calls "skepticism," though it's not clear exactly why he settled on that name. He describes the fourth level in the following way:

> The fourth level is skepticism. You believe the scientific method is the best measure of what is true, and you believe you have a good working grasp of truth, thanks to science, your logic, and your senses. You are arrogant when it comes to dealing with people in levels two and three.

I have much to say about his description of the fourth level of consciousness, but, just so we'll have all of the working parts on the table before we discuss these concerns, we'll look at Adams's conception of the level of awareness of The Avatar himself—level five. Adams says, "The fifth level of awareness is the Avatar. The Avatar understands that the mind is an illusion generator, not a window to reality. The Avatar recognizes science as a belief system, albeit a useful one. An Avatar is aware of God's power as expressed in probability and the inevitable recombination of God consciousness."

So here's my verdict on this in a nutshell: the rank ordering of these levels of awareness is not defensible, and much of what Adams has to say here is inconsistent with some of the other claims he makes in the book.

Adams seems to exhibit a tremendous amount of disdain for people in awareness level four. He leaves no room at all in his system of categories for people who believe in science but do not have disdain for people at earlier stages of the process. He seems to think all stage fours are bound to be arrogant jerks. But, after all, he offers these stages of development as *advances*. So really, what he has to say about the arrogance of people in level four really depends on what he means by *arrogance*. Is it simply that they are aware that they are at a higher stage of development? If so, by his own lights, they are correct about that—that's why they're in the fourth level rather than the third level. If what he means by arrogance here is that people in the fourth level are actually rude to people at the second and third levels, to be sure, there's no need for that, but there's also no reason to believe that is how everyone in level four will behave.

As I mentioned earlier, it is a little strange that he calls people at level four "skeptics." After all, the feature that brings people in that category together is not skepticism, but a belief that logic and the scientific method constitute best epistemic practices—practices that are the most likely to produce true beliefs. If they are skeptical at all about anything, they are skeptical of methods that are less reliable, or perhaps entirely unreliable. So, for example, some people might think that prayer is an effective way to cure someone's cancer. Someone at level four might indeed be skeptical of that claim. This isn't because they are skeptics in general, it's because they believe that some methods are more reliable than others at generating true beliefs.

Here's the rub. When describing the fifth level of awareness, it sure sounds as if he has The Avatar rejecting the existence of objective truth. Recall that he says, "The Avatar understands that the mind is an illusion generator, not a window to reality." So at best, if there is such a thing as truth, the human mind isn't the kind of thing that can get at it.

Right out of the gate, I'll point out that the claim he is making here is self-defeating. In fact, his whole Socratic endeavor up to this point has been an attempt to point The Postman in the direction of truth. All along, he has been asserting that certain facts about metaphysics, epistemology, and even claims about interpersonal relationships *are true.* As I understand it, we're supposed to take his claim that the "mind is an illusion generator" to be a *true claim.* The paradox here is fairly clear. If the mind is a mere illusion generator, than that very mind can't reliably lead us to the conclusion that the mind is an illusion generator. What's more, if there are no objective moral truths, then the claim that "the mind is an illusion generator" can't be true.

There is a further serious inconsistency between two other things that Adams has to say. In the introduction to the book, Adams says, "The central character in *God's Debris* knows everything. Literally everything." What this means is that the Avatar knows every positive fact. Let's assume, since the Avatar explicitly states that he is mortal, that he has a mind. Indeed, Adams claims that both intelligence and awareness belong to the mind, but awareness is a matter of "recognizing your delusions for what they are."

But, the problem is, if the Avatar is truly omniscient *he doesn't have any delusions.* He doesn't believe anything false. What's more, once you introduce an omnipotent entity, you can't also claim that truth is relative. Not if you really want the notion of omniscience to mean anything. If there are no objective truths, *everything is omniscient*. Rocks are omniscient. Tacos are omniscient. If all that's needed for something to be omniscient is that you know every true fact, and it turns out that there are no true facts because there are no such things as objective truths, then omniscience turns out to be a pretty easy standard to meet.

This part of the story should motivate further thought and conversation. The suggestion seems to be that belief in science is just one belief system among many. It's not clear based on this work alone whether this is Adams's own view. In the introduction, he goes out of his way to make it very explicit that the views expressed in the book are not necessarily representative of his own philosophical worldview. So, I'll pin this on The Avatar. I think the view that he is endorsing—the philosophical underpinning of the fifth level of awareness—is tremendously dangerous.

As I've mentioned, the views he's offered are paradoxical when it comes to objective truth. At a very minimum, the repeated success of the scientific method and the rules of logic give us good reason to believe those approaches are superior. If the Avatar were right, there is no reason to believe our science-based current technology (constructed by a belief system that, by his lights, is in no way special) would be any better at, say, agriculture or medicine, than astrology was in the 1600s. That's simply not true. These issues matter. It's not merely theoretical. When people have nonsensical beliefs about epistemic best practices, people die.

I enjoyed *God's Debris*. That said, if you delivered a package to a guy who sold you this bill of goods and you believed he was omniscient, I'd tell you I've got a bridge to sell you.

18
Scott Adams and the Pinocchio Fallacy

David Ramsay Steele

Ever since 1999, many popular writers have been telling us that we're very probably all "living in a simulation." Scott Adams is one of these many. On his Periscopes and on his blog, Scott often returns to this theme. And in *Win Bigly*, he asserts it strongly (p. 35) and actually has an appendix where he tells us how he thinks we can prove it (pp. 267–270).

The idea that we might all be living in a simulation was given its biggest boost by the 1999 movie *The Matrix*. In *The Matrix*, the world we think is real is in fact a gigantic simulation: all the seemingly real facts about the world are not what they appear to be. The human beings who inhabit this world are real, but their bodies are actually being maintained in tanks, and their brains are being fed with information about a physical world which does not truly exist, or if you want to quibble, exists in a form very different from the way it appears. This world can be seen as an involuntary collective delusion, a delusion from which a few have managed to free themselves by "taking the red pill."

The Matrix has some puzzling features which have exercised the minds of fans ever since it appeared. It raises some questions which are not very well answered in the story. For instance, the movie definitely conveys the idea that the electronic "machines" or "Agents" who police the Matrix desperately need the humans, but why they need them is unclear and still controversial among *Matrix* fans. Why keep billions of humans in tanks, at enormous expense?

We're told that the humans are being exploited for the "energy" they provide and they are called "coppertops" (a reference to Duracell batteries). But in terms of literal energy output, measured in watts, this makes no sense. It would not be feasible to recover from the humans more than a minute fraction of the energy required to keep them alive and functioning in their tanks.

This, like many other questions, can be brushed aside with the defense that it's fiction and not everything has to be explained. There are things going on which we're not told about, and which the characters in the story don't know about. Morpheus doesn't explain everything, and the things he does tell Neo and the others, with a great show of certainty, could be his mistaken conclusions (as we eventually learn, at least in a few particulars, they are).

Since the readers of this chapter will all have an IQ above the fortieth percentile, you don't need me to tell you that the point of *The Matrix* is an allegory of the Marxist theory of exploitation and the Marxist theory of ideology. The theory that workers are exploited by capitalists for their "surplus-value" is just as wrongheaded and untenable as the theory that we're all in a computer simulation being exploited for our "energy," but here I'm going to take the *Matrix* story seriously and look at the notion that we're literally "in a simulation."

In *The Matrix*, the humans like Neo, Trinity, and Morpheus really are flesh-and-blood humans. It's just that, before they take the red pill, their bodies are actually inert in tanks, and the world they think they experience is only virtual, a computer simulation. So the human inhabitants of the Matrix do have bodies, and the story requires they must have bodies for the whole shebang to work.

But the "Agents" do seem to be purely electronic entities, able to manifest themselves as fake flesh and blood in the Matrix, but actually without any flesh and blood counterpart. There are also entities like "the Woman in the Red

Dress," who are probably not conscious beings but merely programs inserted into the Matrix, or in this case into a training duplicate of the Matrix. We don't know how many of these entities there are in the actual Matrix.

The version of the "simulation" theory which has now become popular, and which is advocated by Scott Adams, dispenses with the bodies in tanks. It asks us to accept that we are all nothing but pieces of software, chunks of code. So, according to this theory, we're more like the Agents or like the Woman in the Red Dress than like Neo or Trinity. As Scott Adams recognizes, this means that in the simulation theory, we are not merely *in* a simulation (as in *The Matrix*), but we *are* simulations (p. 35).

But is it possible for software code to be conscious? Consider another question. Pinocchio is a boy made entirely of wood. Pinocchio gets the idea he would like to be "a real boy," not just a wooden boy. Could this story possibly be true? Of course not! And why not? Because to develop even a vague hankering to be a real boy entails being conscious. And a block of wood is not the sort of thing that could ever be conscious. A living body containing a nervous system is the sort of thing that could be conscious, and a block of wood is not very much like a living body containing a nervous system.

Why You Cannot Be (in) a Simulation

The theory that "we're all (very probably) living in a simulation" was given a big boost by the philosopher Nick Bostrom. Numerous people outside philosophy have taken Bostrom's argument seriously, and it has spread like a prairie meme among people who write and talk about society, politics, and popular culture.

Bostrom is a serious philosopher and his argument, if you look at it closely, is much more tentative and qualified than the arguments of those, like Scott Adams, who have popularized this approach. I think that Bostrom is mistaken, but I'm not here directly refuting Bostrom, only some of his popularizers like Scott Adams.

The reason you can't be a simulation is because you have conscious experiences. For example, you have sometimes been sick to your stomach and you have sometimes felt euphoric. You have sometimes been sad and sometimes elated. You have sometimes felt itches and sometimes tickles. You have sometimes dreaded something and sometimes eagerly anticipated something. Of course, if you never have experienced anything like those things, you probably are a simulation. You don't know what you're missing, but then, you don't know anything.

Can these conscious experiences be simulated? Of course they can, but a simulation is never the real thing. A simulation of a weather system does not create real thunderstorms or real hurricanes. No one gets wet when a rainstorm is simulated. No trainee pilot has been burned to death in a flight simulator which simulated a crash. In exactly the same way, no one has a conscious experience when a conscious personality is simulated. A *simulation* is not a *replication*. A simulation of consciousness is not consciousness and does not create any consciousness. A simulation of a mind is totally mindless, just like sticks and stones and blocks of wood.

So, can conscious experience be *replicated*? Of course it can. We do this every time we produce a baby. Our babies have conscious experiences, just as we do, and as they grow up, their conscious experiences become even more like ours. We could, perhaps, one day grow brains outside animal bodies, human or non-human, and these brains could have conscious experiences.

It is possible to imagine humans one day designing and creating new kinds of conscious animals "from scratch," so to speak. But these would be real, bodily creatures (literal "creatures" in this case, since we would have created them). Nothing can be conscious without a body; nothing can be conscious except a body.

This isn't at all what the "simulation" proponents like Scott Adams have in mind. What they do have in mind is a situation somewhat like that in *The Matrix*, except that there would be no bodies in tanks. There would be no bodies at all. Instead, conscious thoughts would be generated within electronic computers.

This, I maintain, is quite clearly out of the question. It can never happen and therefore we can never "make progress" towards it. We can be as certain as we can be of anything at all that we are not simulations living in such a simulation world. The world we perceive is real, not fake, and our flesh and blood bodies are parts of this world.

The Simulated World

When popular writers like Scott Adams claim that we're probably living in a simulation, they make a number of assumptions. They take it for granted that the inhabitants of this fake world are just the same kinds of minds, and just the same particular individual personalities, as would inhabit the real world (supposing that the fake world were actually to be not fake but real).

Scott Adams betrays no doubt that the personality of Scott Adams is real, the personality of Donald Trump is real, the personality of Hillary Clinton is real, and the personality of all the minor member of the cast, such as David Ramsay Steele, are real. In this respect, the "simulated" world is just like the world of *The Matrix*: all of the personalities, or at least many of them, do exist, but each is experiencing a fake reality, artificially constructed.

These writers, including Scott, also assume that it's the same, identical fake reality for all the billions of us. Scott doesn't suppose that he's the only "simulated" mind, and that the rest of us are just props in his fake reality (like the Woman in the Red Dress). If he did allow this possibility, it might reduce his incentive to convince us that we're probably living in the fake reality—since he would be trying to convince what amount to little more than figments of his imagination that they are little more than figments of his imagination, and why bother? Especially as Scott keeps reminding us that he has "fuck-you money," is happier and healthier than he has ever been before, and is generally thoroughly chuffed about life.

Scott also doesn't generally doubt that the laws of nature, and the laws of mathematics, are pretty much the same in the fake reality as they would be in the fake reality if it were in fact not fake but real. All proponents of the fake reality theory, and most definitely Scott Adams, argue for the likelihood of the fake reality by appealing to laws of nature and logic (including mathematics) as we discover them in what we take to be reality, which is actually, according to their argument, likely to be fake reality. So they assume that the laws of nature and of logic are the same in the fake reality as they would be in the fake reality if it were not actually fake but real, and presumably also the same as they are in the real reality that underpins the fake reality (for we mustn't forget that for the theory of a fake reality to be true, there has to be a real reality which generates the fake reality).

Scott makes the interesting suggestion that some of the laws of the universe may have been concocted to put limits on what we can find out (because the architects of the simulation face cost constraints). So, we can't travel at above the speed of light, and therefore can't get beyond a certain distance in the universe (*Win Bigly*, p. 268). Scott apparently doesn't notice that if the fake universe we think we're living in includes ad hoc adjustments to physical laws, then the whole argument for thinking we're probably in a simulation is undermined.

What Is Consciousness?

Consciousnesss involves inner, subjective experience. Here are some examples of conscious states:

- **feeling happy**
- **feeling miserable**
- **feeling pain**
- **feeling an itch**
- **feeling a tickle**
- **feeling apprehensive because there is an earthquake**
- **feeling apprehensive for no apparent reason**

- believing something (feeling convinced that something is true)
- believing that the world we live in might be some kind of fake construction
- hoping that things will get better
- fearing that things will get worse
- feeling hungry or thirsty
- feeling that something is meaningful
- feeling that something is not just meaningful but very important

No one, at the present time, has the *slightest* idea how to design a computer or any other machine that experiences any of these states, *except* by reproducing or somehow reconstructing a living animal with a brain. And, related to that, no one has the *slightest* idea how to design a computer that can understand what it's doing or can attribute meaning to anything.

Now, you might raise the objection that these inner, subjective states are of no importance. If we can construct a simulation of interacting conscious minds, what does it matter that it's just a simulation, that there is actually no consciousness?

Well, suppose I were to tell you that I'm about to give you an injection. After that injection, your body will continue to behave, so far as anyone can observe, just like it does now. It will talk in coherent sentences and give the appearance of expressing emotions, but really it will be bereft of emotions or of any conscious feelings. Your inner subjective state will be that of someone in a deep coma—that is, you will not have any inner subjective state. You will never again have any *experiences*, even though your body will continue to behave normally.

Assuming you understand me and believe what I'm telling you, you will view the injection as lethal. I will be threatening you with murder. From the moment of that injection, you'll be dead meat, even though your body will continue to operate normally. You will be legally alive but there will be no "you" any more.

So, *nothing is more important than consciousness*. Nothing could ever be more vital than consciousness, because without consciousness nothing can have any meaning. Paraphrasing the King James version of 1 Corinthians 13, we may say:

> Though I speak with the tongues of men and of angels, and have not *consciousness*, I am become as sounding brass or a tinkling cymbal.

That would indeed be precisely the death of being turned into a mindless robot.

However, the question of the vital importance of consciousness is, strictly speaking, a side-issue. More fundamental to the argument is the fact that you are conscious, and you know you are conscious, whether or not you or I judge this to be of any importance. So it doesn't matter *for the argument* whether it's important that you're conscious. All that matters is that your being conscious proves that you cannot be a simulation.

But now you might say, granted that no one has the slightest idea how to make a machine, other than an animal body, have conscious experiences, who's to say that some way of doing this might not be discovered, perhaps thousands of years from now? The quick answer is that we can't rule out this possibility, but that the making of an artificial consciousness will require the arrangement of matter and energy in a particular way, in effect the creation of a new kind of conscious body—even thought it might, conceivably, be a conscious body based on a different kind of chemistry—and that this arrangement of matter and energy can't possibly be simply lines of code, because simulation can never amount to replication.

Scott refers to "the simple fact that we will someday be able to create software simulations that believe they are real creatures" (p. 35). But this "simple fact" is a simple falsehood; the simple fact is that we will never be able to make software that believes anything at all. Believing, like understanding, is just one of those things that computers can't do (see Hubert Dreyfus, *What Computers Still Can't Do*).

How Some People Typically "Argue" for the Simulated World

When popular writers explain to us why they think we're probably living in a simulation, they all say more or less the same thing. First, they soften us up by suggesting that computers are "intelligent," and as they get better and better, they will become more and more "intelligent."

However, the word "intelligent" is ambiguous. Deep Blue, the program that won a chess game against Garry Kasparov, was intelligent in one sense but not in another. Deep Blue had no inkling of what it was doing. Deep Blue, just like a ten-dollar pocket calculator, had not the faintest notion of what was going on. It understood nothing. It was unable to see meaning in anything. It had no idea it was playing a game, and no notion of what playing a game means.

The use of the term "processing power" is then brought in to add to the ambiguity. The inattentive reader may pick up the idea that there is some general thing called "processing power" which can produce consciousness if there is enough of it. Computers do processing and so does the brain, right? But then, so does a sewage treatment plant and so does a soap factory, and we don't expect either of them to create consciousness, no matter how much processing they do.

We may be tempted to think like this: computation is somewhat analogous to thought, and thought is a conscious process, therefore computation is close enough to a kind of consciousness. But no amount of computation can produce consciousness. We do not know of any "processing power" that could ever produce thought.

We will then be told that we can assume "substrate-independence" meaning that consciousness doesn't depend on any particular type of physical system. Here two confusions are combined. First, the fact that we don't know enough to rule out the possibility that some other substrate might work is rephrased to suggest that we know that some other substrate might work.

Second, the issue of whether there might possibly be a different kind of substrate is confused with the issue of whether a particular system picked at random might be that different kind of substrate.

Sometimes confusion is piled upon confusion when it is suggested that the issue is between carbon-based systems (like us) and silicon-based systems (like computers). A computer could be built using carbon instead of silicon, and it would be equally incapable of consciousness or thought. Carbon has amazing properties unlike any other element, which is why chemistry is divided into two great kingdoms: organic (involving carbon) and inorganic (without carbon). To surmise that life above a certain level of complexity might just *have* to be carbon-based is not at all crazy.

But more crucially, let's suppose that one day we can discover, or create, a physical body based on silicon instead of carbon, and this body is conscious. This is conceivable—meaning only that we don't yet know enough to rule it out. Such a body would not be a computer, and the conceivability of such a body has no bearing on the fact that a computer can't be conscious.

(Here, to avoid unnecessary verbal complications, I'm skipping over the fact that according to the quaint argot of "artificial intelligence," *any* object, such as a screwdriver or a paperweight, or a brain, is *defined* as being "a digital computer." Here I'm following ordinary speech, where "a computer" is something like my laptop, whereas a screwdriver, a paperweight, or a human brain are not "computers.")

We can transfer the substrate 'argument' to the case of Pinocchio. Since we can't rule out the possibility that consciousness could have a different substrate, therefore (logical slip) we can't rule out that possibility that a block of wood could become conscious, and therefore (another logical slip) a block of wood could "in principle" be conscious. We seem to have proved that a block of wood could do the trick as well! But we know that can't be right, because we happen to know that the idea of a block of wood becoming conscious is totally silly. We have been handed something that looks a bit like an argument but is actually bogus through and through.

As far as we can tell, the cosmos is empty of consciousness except as this has arisen in animal brains. But this, of course, doesn't show that consciousness *couldn't* arise in a different physical system (or hasn't already). So, we may speculate, there could be consciousness arising from a different type of physical system, perhaps very different in some ways from the animal brains we know about.

In *Whipping Star* (spoiler alert), Frank Herbert supposes that stars are conscious and that they can intervene in the interactions of other conscious beings such as ourselves. We can't prove this isn't true, but I suspect that if civilization and science survive for a couple of hundred more years, we will establish the physical essentials of consciousness, and thus be able to prove that stars can't possibly be conscious.

We do not know of any consciousness except in animal bodies. At one time people attributed consciousness to natural forces, but we now know this to be false. At one time people believed they had observed ghosts or other disembodied consciousnesses (though in many versions the ghosts have bodies of sorts). But we have learned that ghosts, like the Martian canals, or like the Loch Ness Monster, or like the spontaneous generation of living organisms from dirt, though once frequently observed, simply cease to be observed when the observation procedures are tightened up.

Consciousness is a real physical property produced by a physical system. Consider any other property which can be produced by a physical system—say, stickiness (I mean literal stickiness, like the stickiness of Scotch tape). Can we write a computer program that would produce stickiness? No, never. Stickiness arises because of the specific structure of certain kinds of molecules. We can simulate stickiness in a computer program, that is, we can generate mathematical models of physical bodies which are sticky—they behave in the simulation as if they were sticky. But they are not really sticky. It's no use saying that if computing power can be increased billions-fold, we will one day be able to get stickiness out of software. This is forever an absurdity. We may, of course, find or create sticky physical substances that have not existed before, and no doubt there are ways to do this. But we have to step outside the software to do it. We are then no longer simulating; we are replicating.

As it is with stickiness, so it is with consciousness. We may, perhaps, be able to bring into being new types of physical systems, in some ways radically unlike the animals we're familiar with, which will be conscious. The argument that we don't know that today's animals are the only things which can be conscious points to the possibility of different types of physical systems which might be conscious; it doesn't point to the possibility that software might become conscious.

One More Thing

If we did create a new type of physical system which could be conscious, it doesn't follow that we would inflict upon these creatures a purposely false understanding of their place in the world.

We've seen that the arguments for software becoming conscious are more rhetorical than reasonable, and that the idea is, when all's said and done, more than a bit fanciful. But there is another point we can raise against it. That is the question of the motive for any advanced civilization to create such a "simulated" fake world. Just as fans of *The Matrix* have trouble with the motive, so the theorists of a simulated world have trouble with the motive.

To condemn millions of minds to living in a fake world is obviously immoral, especially if that fake world is full of terrible suffering (real suffering, actual agony, not simulated suffering, which would be no suffering at all) which could easily have been eliminated by writing the program differently. And if it were possible to create real minds within software, then such minds would have their own way of experiencing the world, their own emotions, objectives, and sensibilities, no doubt dramatically different from those of mammals like us. There would be a moral imperative to provide conditions conducive to the flourishing and fulfillment of such software creatures (or not to create them in the first place).

No one will ever be able to create conscious software. But just supposing they could, it would be morally wrong for them to do it in such a way that these new software-minds were trapped in a fake world of illusion, instead of being able to reach out and grasp reality, as we do.

Bibliography

Adams, Scott. 1996. *The Dilbert Principle: A Cubicle's-Eye View of Bosses, Meetings, Management Fads, and Other Workplace Afflictions*. HarperBusiness.

———. 1996. *Dogbert's Top Secret Management Handbook: As Told to Scott Adams*. HarperBusiness.

———. 1997. *The Dilbert Future: Thriving on Stupidity in the 21st Century*. HarperBusiness.

———. 1998. *The Joy of Work: Dilbert's Guide to Finding Happiness at the Expense of Your Co-Workers*. HarperBusiness.

———. 2001. *God's Debris: A Thought Experiment*. Andrews McMeel.

———. 2002. *Dilbert and the Way of the Weasel: A Guide to Outwitting Your Boss, Your Coworkers, and the Other Pants-Wearing Ferrets in Your Life*. HarperBusiness.

———. 2004. *The Religion War*. Andrews McMeel.

———. 2007. *Stick to Drawing Comics, Monkey Brain! Cartoonist Ignores Helpful Advice*. Penguin.

———. 2013. *How to Fail at Almost Everything and Still Win Big: Kind of the Story of My Life*. Penguin.

———. 2017. *Win Bigly: Persuasion in a World Where Facts Don't Matter*. Penguin.

Allen, Jonathan, and Amy Parnes. 2017. *Shattered: Inside Hillary Clinton's Doomed Campaign*. Crown.

Ariely, Dan. 2009. *Predictably Irrational: The Hidden Forces that Shape Our Decisions*. HarperCollins.

Aristotle. 1989. *Prior Analytics*. Hackett.

———. 1999. *The Metaphysics*. Penguin.

———. 2004. *Rhetoric*. Dover.

———. 2006. *Nicomachean Ethics*. Clarendon.

———. 2006. *On Rhetoric: A Theory of Civic Discourse*. Oxford University Press.

Bartley, William Warren, III. 1984 [1962]. *The Retreat to Commitment*. Open Court.

Bateson, Gregory. 2000 [1972]. *Steps to an Ecology of Mind: Collected Essays in Anthropology, Psychiatry, Evolution, and Epistemology*. University of Chicago Press.

Beauvoir, Simone de. 2011 [1949]. *The Second Sex*. Vintage.

———. 1976. *The Ethics of Ambiguity*. Citadel.

Bernays, Edward. 1928. *Propaganda*. Liveright.

Bostrom, Nick. 2003. Are We Living in *The Matrix*? The Simulation Argument. In Glenn Yeffeth, ed., *Taking the Red Pill: Science, Philosophy, and Religion in The Matrix*. BenBella.

———. 2005. Why Make a Matrix? And Why You Might Be in One. In William Irwin, ed., *More Matrix and Philosophy: Revolutions and Reloaded Decoded*. Open Court.

Brafman, Ori, and Rom Brafman. 2008. *Sway: The Irresistible Pull of Irrational Behavior*. Doubleday.

Brennan, Jason. 2016. Against Democracy. *The National Interest* (September 6th).

———. 2016. *Against Democracy*. Princeton University Press.

Brewster, Sir David. 1855. *Memoirs of the Life, Writings, and Discoveries of Sir Isaac Newton*. Constable.

Brown, Derren. 2007. *Tricks of the Mind*. Channel 4.

———. 2017. *Happy: Why More or Less Anything Is Absolutely Fine*. TW Adult.

Buffett, Warren. 2012. *Tap Dancing to Work: Warren Buffett on Practically Everything, 1966–2013*. Penguin.

Camus, Albert. 1961 [1945]. *Resistance, Rebellion, and Death*. [Includes *Letters to a German Friend*.] Knopf.

———. 1991 [1955]. *The Myth of Sisyphus and Other Essays*. Vintage.

———. 2013 [1942]. *The Outsider*. Penguin.

Carnegie, Dale. 1981 [1936]. *How to Win Friends and Influence People*. Simon and Schuster.

Cassidy, John. 2013. The Reinhart and Rogoff Controversy: A Summing Up. *The New Yorker* (April 26th).

Cernovich, Mike. 2015. *Gorilla Mindset*. Archangel Ink.

Chakhotin, Sergei. 1971 [1940]. *The Rape of the Masses: The Psychology of Totalitarian Political Propaganda*. Haskell House.

Bibliography

Chomsky, Noam. 2002. *Media Control: The Spectacular Achievements of Propaganda*. Seven Stories.

Cialdini, Robert. 2012. *Influence: Science and Practice—The Comic*. Illustrated by Nathan Lueth. Writers of the Round Table.

———. 2013 [1984]. *Influence: Science and Practice*. Fifth edition. Pearson's.

———. 2016. *Pre-Suasion: A Revolutionary Way to Influence and Persuade*. Simon and Schuster.

Cipolla, Carlo M. 1987. The Basic Laws of Human Stupidity. *Whole Earth Review*.

———. 2011. *The Basic Laws of Human Stupidity*. Il Mulino.

Coulter, Ann. 2016. *In Trump We Trust: E Pluribus Awesome!* Penguin.

Crain, Caleb. 2016. The Case Against Democracy. *The New Yorker* (November 7th).

Dreyfus, Hubert L. 1992. *What Computers Still Can't Do: A Critique of Artificial Reason*. MIT Press.

Ellis, Ralph, and Natika Newton. 2010. *How the Mind Uses the Brain: To Move the Body and Image the Universe*. Open Court.

Ellul, Jacques. 1973 [1962]. *Propaganda: The Formation of Men's Attitudes*. Vintage.

Estlund, David. 2008. *Democratic Authority: A Philosophical Framework*. Princeton University Press.

Fowler, Erika Franklin, Travis M. Ridout, and Michael M. Franz. 2017. Political Advertising in 2016: The Presidential Election as Outlier? [The Wesleyan Study.] *The Forum: A Journal of Applied Research in Contemporary Politics* 14:4.

Friend, Stacie. 2007. Fictional Characters. *Philosophy Compass* 2:2.

Gass, Robert H., and John S. Seiter. 2013. *Persuasion: Social Influence and Compliance Gaining*. Routledge.

Gigerenzer, Gerd. 2008. *Rationality for Mortals: How People Cope with Uncertainty*. Oxford University Press.

———. 2015. *Simply Rational: Decision Making in the Real World*. Oxford University Press.

Gigerenzer, Gerd, Peter M. Todd, and the ABC Research Group. 2000. *Simple Heuristics that Make Us Smart*. Oxford University Press.

Gini, Al. 2001. *My Job, My Self: Work and the Creation of the Modern Individual*. Routledge.

Goldstein, Noah J., Steve J. Martin, and Robert B. Cialdini. 2008. *Yes! 50 Scientifically Proven Ways to Be Persuasive*. Simon and Schuster.

Gopnik, Alison. 2009. *The Philosophical Baby: What Children's Minds Tell Us about Truth, Love, and the Meaning of Life*. Farrar, Straus, and Giroux.

Gopnik, Alison, and Andrew N. Meltzoff. 1998. *Words, Thoughts, and Theories*. MIT Press.

Gopnik, Alison, Andrew N. Meltzoff, and Patricia K. Kuhl. 2001 [1999]. *The Scientist in the Crib: What Early Learning Tells Us about the Mind*. HarperCollins.

Harwood, Robin. 1998. More Votes for PhD's. *Journal of Social Philosophy* 29.

Herndon, Thomas, Michael Ash, and Robert Pollin. 2013. Does High Public Debt Consistently Stifle Economic Growth? A Critique of Reinhart and Rogoff. *Political Economy Research Institute* Working Paper #322 (April).

Herrick, Paul. 2015. *Think with Socrates: An Introduction to Critical Thinking*. Oxford University Press.

Irwin, William, ed. 2002. *The Matrix and Philosophy: Welcome to the Desert of the Real*. Open Court.

Kahneman, Daniel. 2011. *Thinking, Fast and Slow*. Farrar, Straus, and Giroux.

Kripke, Saul A. 1980. *Naming and Necessity*. Harvard University Press.

Krugman, Paul. 2013. Reinhart-Rogoff Continued. *New York Times* (April 6th).

LaBossiere, Michael C. 2013. *76 Fallacies*. Michael LaBossiere.

Lawrence, Matt. 2004. *Like a Splinter in Your Mind: The Philosophy Behind the Matrix Trilogy*. Wiley-Blackwell.

Le Bon, Gustave. 2002 [1895]. *The Crowd: A Study of the Popular Mind*. Dover.

Lebesque, Morvan. 1963. *Albert Camus par Lui-Même*. Éditions du Seuil.

Lewis, David K. 2001. *On the Plurality of Worlds*. Wiley-Blackwell.

Lifton, Robert Jay. 1989 [1961]. *Thought Reform and the Pschology of Totalism: A Study of "Brainwashing" in China*. University of North Carolia Press.

Lumley, F.E. 1933. *The Propaganda Menace*. Appleton.

Mackay, Charles. 2009 [1841]. *Extraordinary Popular Delusions and the Madness of Crowds*. Wilder.

Morreall, John, ed. 1986. *The Philosophy of Laughter and Humor*. Albany: State University of New York Press.

Mill, John Stuart. 1991 [1861]. *Considerations on Representative Government*. Prometheus.

Nussbaum, Martha. 2010. *Not for Profit: Why Democracy Needs the Humanities*. Princeton University Press.

Marcus, Gary. 2008. *Kluge: The Haphazard Construction of the Human Mind*. Houghton Mifflin.

McPhail, Clark. 1991. *The Myth of the Madding Crowd*. De Gruyter,

Miller, David. 1994. *Critical Rationalism: A Restatement and Defence*. Open Court

Nye, R.A. 1975. *The Origins of Crowd Psychology: Gustave Le Bon and the Crisis of Mass Democracy in the Third Republic*. Sage.

Peale, Norman Vincent. 2003 [1952]. *The Power of Positive Thinking*. Touchstone.

Pellegrini, Mark, Timothy Lim, and Brett R. Smith. 2017. *Thump: The First Bundred Days*. Post Hill Press.

Percival, Ray Scott. 2012. *The Myth of the Closed Mind: Understanding Why and How People Are Rational*. Open Court.

Plato. 1997. *Complete Works*. Hackett.

———. 2007. *The Republic*. Penguin.

Popper, Karl R. 2002 [1963]. *Conjectures and Refutations: The Growth of Scientific Knowledge*. Routledge.

———. 1979 [1972]. *Objective Knowledge: An Evolutionary Approach*. Oxford University Press.

———. 1992 [1983]. *Realism and the Aim of Science: From the Postscript to The Logic of Scientific Discovery*. Routledge.

Pratkanis, Anthony R., and Elliot Aronson. 2001 [1992]. *Age of Propaganda: The Everyday Use and Abuse of Persuasion*. Holt.

Reich, Wilhelm. 1980 [1933]. *The Mass Psychology of Fascism*. Farrar, Straus, and Giroux.

Reinhart, Carmen M., and Kenneth S. Rogoff. 2010. Growth in a Time of Debt. *American Economic Review* 100:2.

Sargant, William. 1959 [1957]. *Battle for the Mind: A Physiology of Conversion and Brainwashing*. Pan.

Sartre, Jean-Paul. 1993 [1943]. *Being and Nothingness: A Phenomenological Essay on Ontology*. Simon and Schuster.

Schumacher E.F. 1980. *Good Work*. Harper Collins.

Searle, John R. 1992. *The Rediscovery of the Mind*. MIT Press.
———. 1997. *The Mystery of Consciousness*. New York Review.
Sirkin, Harold L., Justin R. Rose, and Michael Zinser. 2012. *The US Manufacturing Renaissance: How Shifting Global Economics Are Creating an American Comeback*. A free download from Knowledge@Wharton.
Somin, Ilya. 2016. Democracy vs. Epistocracy. *Washington Post* (September 3rd).
Stanley, Jason. 2015. *How Propaganda Works*. Princeton University Press.
Terkel, Studs. 1974. *Working: People Talk about What They Do All Day and How They Feel about What They Do*. New Press.
Trotter, Wilfred. 2009 [1916]. *Instincts of the Herd in Peace and War*. Cornell University Library.
Trump. Donald J. 2015 [1987]. *The Art of the Deal*. Random House.
Van Inwagen, Peter. 1977. Creatures of Fiction. *American Philosophical Quarterly* 14:4.
Wolff, Michael. 2018. *Fire and Fury: Inside the Trump White House*. Holt.
Zaller, John R. 1992. *The Nature and Origins of Mass Opinion*. Cambridge University Press.
Zalta, Edward N. 2003. Referring to Fictional Characters. *Dialectica* 57:2.

Author Bios

ROBERT ARP works for the US Department of Defense and has many interests in philosophy. See robertarp.com. A time that he used the power of persuasion—as opposed to good reasoning—to gain a benefit for himself was when he was a junior in high school running for the coveted senior-year position of Student Council President. He had dozens of pointed pencils made that read, "Be Sharp, Vote for Arp" and handed out dozens of buttons that read, "I'm Sharp, I'm Voting for Arp." Of course, his button read, "I'm Arp, but I'm Still Voting for Arp." He also had stickers made, and placed them on lockers, in lockers, under lockers, and over lockers . . . He even placed them on the back of bathroom stall doors and on the inside of the urinals.

Everywhere he went, he would unabashedly proclaim, "Be Sharp, Vote for Arp" so that students began echoing the slogan back at him in between class periods. During the big debate between the three candidates in the gym, at which the entire school was present, he purposely chose to go last. When asked the first question by the Principal, who was acting as moderator, "Mr. Arp, if elected, what will you do to better the high school community?" he paused for an uncomfortable amount of time, then leaned into the mic and responded in a deep voice, "NO COMMENT." A mass hush fell upon the space. A split second later, several gasps were heard. Heads that were looking anywhere other than at the stage snapped forward. And all eyes were definitely on Rob. He continued: "... Which is what you will NEVER hear when I'm Student Council President!" People started clapping and cheering, hooting and hollering, and whooping and whistling as Rob laid out his plans to do X, Y, and Z next year for the school—plans that would never materialize because they were so unbelievably batshit crazy you'd have to be smoking salvia to think that they would, despite the fact that he did indeed win the presidency. He had "Mr. President" stitched on his school sweater the day before school started his senior year— what a cocky bastard . . .

ADAM BARKMAN is Professor of Philosophy and Chair of the Philosophy Department at Redeemer University College. He has written a crapload of books, but nothing as cool as a Dilbert book. A time he used his power of persuasion—as opposed to good reasoning—to gain a benefit is when he convinced his wife to marry him.

RICHARD BILSKER is Professor of Philosophy and Social Sciences at the College of Southern Maryland, where he has taught since 1995. He has broad teaching and research interests in philosophy, political science, sociology, psychology, and the humanities. His books include *On Bergson* and *On Jung*. His articles and book reviews have appeared in *Teaching Philosophy*, *Humanity and Society*, *Idealistic Studies*, *ephemera*, and *Hyle*. His hobbies include tabletop roleplaying games, single-malt scotch (especially during election season), Doctor Who, and wondering whether he would be better off if he were a cat.

ALEXANDER CHRISTIAN is the assistant director of the Düsseldorf Center for Logic and Philosophy of Science and a research fellow at the Chair of Theoretical Philosophy at Heinrich Heine University in Düsseldorf. He has interests in general philosophy of science (demarcation problem, values in science) and research ethics (scientific misconduct and questionable research practices in medical research). A time that he used the power of persuasion—as opposed to good reasoning—to gain a benefit for himself was when he was fifteen years old and saw that one of his female classmates was struggling to fake a sick note for the upcoming gym class. He persuaded her to buy him a bag of crisps and a diet coke in exchange for a well-written sick note. After looking at the note, their sports teacher busted out laughing. Handing the sick note back to his student, he told her: "I hope your prostate problems are no hindrance to today's 5k cross run."

CHARLENE ELSBY is the Philosophy Program Director and Assistant Professor of Philosophy at Purdue Fort Wayne, researching Aristotle and Realist Phenomenology. A time that she used the power of persuasion—as opposed to good reasoning—to gain a benefit for herself was applying to her first office job. And when she says "persuasion," she means "pie." She brought a pie to the interview, just to let everyone know that were she to be hired, there would be more pies to come. She got that job, and many a pie were had by all.

GALEN FORESMAN is Associate Professor of Philosophy at North Carolina Agricultural and Technical State University, home to the Greensboro Four and the Greensboro Uprising. Although he often confuses his powers of persuasion with his magic abilities—or was it the other way around?—he's certain that the predictive power of these filters will sort it out for him in the future. Surely, confirmation bias and cognitive dissonance will ascertain the appropriate distinction for us all . . . until something better comes along.

RICHARD GREENE is Professor of Philosophy at Weber State University, Chair of the board of the Intercollegiate Ethics Bowl, and Director of the Richard Richards Institute for Ethics. He has edited or co-edited many books; his latest is *Twin Peaks and Philosophy: That's Damn Fine Philosophy!* A time that he used the power of persuasion—as opposed to good reasoning—to gain a benefit for himself was when he convinced his family that no one owns just one ukulele. Seven ukes later (and counting!) his persuasive skills are still in full force and paying dividends.

ENZO GUERRA is an independent scholar who has published on ethics and comparative religion. A time that he used the power of persuasion—as opposed to good reasoning—to gain a benefit for himself was when, as an undergrad, he convinced a mere stranger on a bus that he was a visiting international doctoral student. He felt warm and fuzzy inside being thought more important than he was.

SANDRA HANSMANN is an Associate Professor at the University of Texas Rio Grande Valley. Her interests are focused on women's issues in the areas of disability, health, and gender-based discrimination and violence. She's also interested in the use of social media in counseling and disability studies. A time when Sandra used the power of persuasion—as opposed to good reasoning—to gain a benefit for herself was when she convinced a men's rights activist that his "red pill" wasn't really red, but pink, having decided she'd rather argue about that issue than hear the "involuntarily celibate" asshole continue yammering about the matriarchal world takeover.

CYNTHIA JONES is an Associate Professor of Philosophy and the Director of the Office for Victim Advocacy and Violence Prevention at the University of Texas Rio Grande Valley, where she also directs the Gelman Constitutional Scholars Program and is the past director and founder of the University's Ethics Center.

From the Desk of the CFO: Performance Review: **JOHN V. KAR-AVITIS**. "John needs to be mindful of his demeanor when he works with others. [Many managers and co-workers] have expressed that John sometimes comes across like [*sic*] he was lecturing or explaining the obvious . . . that he knows best and we are all wrong. John needs work [*sic*] on his communication skills as he is coming across sounding accusational, combative and/or condescending. He talks too much without . . ."
Overall Rating of Employee: Meets Expectations.
Employee's Response: You meant "accusatory." There is no such word as "accusational." And you're welcome.

CHRISTOPHER KETCHAM
DOCTORATE: UNIVERSITY OF TEXAS AT AUSTIN
TEACHES BUSINESS AND ETHICS AT UNIVERSITY OF
HOUSTON DOWNTOWN

DOES RESEARCH IN:
- Risk management
- Applied ethics
- Social justice
- East-West comparative philosophy
- Emmanuel Levinas and Gabriel Marcel

IMPORTANT TO KNOW, UNDERSTAND, AND BELIEVE!
- There is no collision
- We will make Amerika greet again
- Vlad Emir Puttin is a nice man
- Little hanz mean big ideas
- Forget all that, just vote earlie and offen
- Oh, and bild the WALL E

IN CONCUSSION:
- No fake climit change
- Dig more cole; make more coke
- Robit Arp is fake news

ELLIOT KNUTHS is a Juris Doctor Candidate at Northwestern University's Pritzker School of Law. His philosophical interests lie primarily in metaphysics and philosophy of religion. A time that Knuths used the power of persuasion—as opposed to good reasoning—to gain a benefit for himself occurred when he was still in high school. During homecoming week, dressed only in a toga (other people were wearing togas, too—he wasn't *that* weird), he used impassioned rhetoric to convince his principal to interrupt the last five minutes of class and play "Shout" over the intercom system, thus emulating a famous scene from *Animal House*. Although this interlude probably wasn't very educational and may even have been seen by some as a waste of time, Knuths found it amusing and remembers it better than whichever class it cut short.

ROB LUZECKY is a lecturer at Purdue Fort Wayne. He finds the life of the cubical worker to be anathema, and counts himself lucky to have an office with four walls and a door. The best part of his day is when he gets to lecture about the coming revolution, aesthetics, and other cool topics to those who have not yet been beaten into submission by vaguely psychotic middle-managers. While he believes it's entirely reasonable to demand that the world be a better place, he finds that people are more easily convinced of the validity of this claim when they are looking at pretty pictures. He has co-written numerous book chapters on popular culture and philosophy, and co-edited *Amy Schumer and Philosophy: Brainwreck!* (2018).

DANIEL MIORI is a Physician Assistant and author who has occupied a space at the curious intersection of medicine, ethics, and philosophy for the past decade. Widely disregarded as a talentless hack, he managed to use the power of persuasion—as opposed to good reasoning—to gain a benefit for himself when he somehow coerced Dan Yim, Galen Foresman, and Robert Arp into including his chapter, which he wanted to call "Epistemology, The Scientific Method, and Why Scott Adams Is Stupid," in their otherwise informative and entertaining book. He probably has video of them peeing on hookers or something like that.

RAY SCOTT PERCIVAL is the author of the critically acclaimed *The Myth of the Closed Mind: Understanding Why and How People are Rational* (2012). A time that he used the power of persuasion—as opposed to good reasoning—to gain a benefit for himself and his friends was as a teenager under the mesmerising influence of space aliens. Percival persuaded his dilatory friends to attend a rock concert featuring the charismatic Space Preachers, by telling each of his friends in rapid succession, starting with the most gullible and working up to the most skeptical, that all the others he had spoken too had already enthusiastically committed to going. Within his esoteric circle, Percival baptised this tool of persuasion FEARISMM—"the fear of exclusion by accelerated rapid incremental social momentum manoeuvre." Percival later suffered much anguish over his deviation from his Socratic ideal of being guided by sweet truth. Taking pity on him, the space aliens assured Percival that Adams is at least partly correct: sometimes, in the short-run, facts don't matter—just what people believe. His only real consolation was that they all had a rock'n'roll time.

RACHEL ROBISON-GREENE is a Post Doctoral Fellow at Utah State University. Rachel has edited or co-edited twelve volumes in the Popular Culture and Philosophy series, the latest being *The Handmaid's Tale and Philosophy* (2018). A time that she used the power of persuasion—as opposed to good reasoning—to gain a benefit for herself was to convince her family that getting a new puppy really was a good idea. She was wrong. She should have stuck with good reasoning.

JULIETTA RIVERA, who did the illustration for Chapter 9, is not only a comic-strip creator but also an artist in ceramic and paint, as well as an art teacher. She is the owner and operator of the Gallo Gallery and Studios.

BEN SAUNDERS is Associate Professor in the Department of Politics and International Relations at the University of Southampton. His primary interests are in democratic theory and the permissible limits of state action. He's not sure that he's ever successfully used the power of persuasion—as opposed to good reasoning—for anything. If he possessed such power, he'd probably get a job in sales or marketing, instead of doing real work.

DAVID RAMSAY STEELE is an interstellar celebrity author whose books sell far too many copies to be listed in mainstream bestseller charts. He wrote the iconoclastic study of George Orwell, *Orwell Your Orwell: A Worldview on the Slab* (2017). His other books include *Atheism Explained: From Folly to Philosophy* (2008) and *From Marx to Mises: Post-Capitalist Society and the Challenge of Economic Calculation* (1992). A time he used high-powered persuasion technique to gain a benefit for himself was when he persuaded the Nobel Committee to award him the Nobel Peace Prize. What? Yes, well, as Scott Adams rightly points out, it would be unreasonable to expect persuasion to work one hundred percent of the time.

ANDY WIBLE is a full-time instructor at Muskegon Community College. He has interests in business ethics, biomedical ethics, and queer studies. A time that he used the power of persuasion—as opposed to good reasoning—to gain a benefit for himself was when he was in college and worked going door to door collecting money for a group called Citizens Action. He got paid half of what he collected. Andy went to a house and talked to a lonely young goth kid named Jonathan, he said his parents were not home. Andy returned two hours later and Jonathan's mother opened the door. Andy said that he had talked to Jonathan earlier. She said, "Oh you're a friend of Jonathan, come on in." Andy said nothing and followed her into the kitchen. She gave him a glass of milk and some cookies. Her husband came in and introduced himself. Andy then gave his plea for money. The couple looked at each other and shook their heads. The husband went and got a check for twenty dollars, but Andy didn't get a refill of his milk.

IVAN WOLFE teaches English at Arizona State University and has a PhD in Rhetoric from the University of Texas, Austin. A time Ivan used the power of persuasion—as opposed to good reasoning—to gain a benefit for himself was—well, Ivan tries to always use good reasoning when doing persuasion with adults (it's possible to do both!). However, he uses persuasion that quite often lacks good reasoning when dealing with his many, many children, and the examples of that are both too numerous to mention and also likely too familiar to anyone out there that is or has been a parent (and if you, like one young soon-to-be parent Ivan talked to recently, think you will be the exception and always use good reasoning when trying to persuade your children, the universe laughs at you).

DANIEL YIM is Department Chair and Professor of Philosophy at Bethel University. He has interests in early modern philosophy, the intersections of race, gender, and sexuality, the philosophy of popular culture, and the epistemology of self-deception.

Index